Department of the Environment
Welsh Office

WATER RESOURCES AND SUPPLY: AGENDA FOR ACTION

LONDON : The
October 1996

ISBN 0 11 753299 1

 Recycled Paper

Et plui super unam civitatem

'I would send rain upon one city'. In the Latin, these words from the biblical[1] prophecy of Amos adorned the seal of one of the very earliest private water companies, which in 1613 had completed the then monumental and far-sighted task of constructing an aqueduct some 40 miles long to bring water by gravity to the City of London. Written some 2,700 years ago, these words remind us across the ages of the fundamental dependence of water supply, to a whole community, upon rainfall.

The biblical passage continues 'and send no rain upon another city'. The drought of 1995 which affected large parts of England and Wales, and which has continued into 1996 in many areas, focused attention on water resources. The question also arose of whether this drought is a manifestation of climate change. This was the background to the commissioning of this paper on the arrangements for securing sufficient supplies in the longer term.

The paper confirms that the framework for those arrangements is sound. The water companies have the duty to maintain supplies. The industry's three regulators have the duty of ensuring that it is carried out properly. Companies and regulators alike are charged with taking full account of the environmental impacts of their actions so that water – in its nature a renewable resource – is managed sustainably. The Government retains responsibility for the legislative and policy framework within which the companies and regulators operate. This paper contributes to the discharge of that responsibility. It sets out a framework of policy and strategy within which the regulators' and companies' duties should be discharged so as to ensure that the water we need in the longer term is provided effectively, efficiently, and in an environmentally sustainable way.

The paper identifies actions to be taken by water companies, the regulators and by Government. Prominent amongst these are steps which should be taken to build upon work on climate change scenarios, such as that which informed the report of the Department of the Environment's Climate Change Impacts Review Group which was published in July.[2]

The paper also draws attention to the various contributions which water companies, manufacturers of water-using equipment and water consumers can all make to the sustainable management of water resources through water conservation. Just as, in the quotation, the rain falls on a city – a community of people, so sustainable development is a matter for each and every one of us as individual members of the community. This *Agenda for Action* is for us all.

John Gummer
Secretary of State for the Environment

William Hague
Secretary of State for Wales

---

1 Amos 4.7.

2 *Review of the Potential Effects of Climate Change in the United Kingdom*. HMSO, London, July 1996.

Contents

Executive Summary 1

Introduction 6

The Overall Context: Water Use and
Sustainable Development 8

The Legal and Regulatory Framework

Preamble 11
Duty to maintain water supply 11
Quality of water supplies 12
Water use 12
Water resource management 12
Environmental duties 12
Summary 13
Amendment of the legal framework 13

Rainfall and Climate Change

Droughts 14
Rainfall and water resource yields 14
Climate change 15

Demand for Public Water Supplies

Past and current demand 17
Forecasts of future demand 18
Climate change 19

Demand Management: Introduction . . 21

Increasing Efficiency of Use

Provision of more water-efficient equipment and
fittings 22
Proposed regulatory action in respect of fittings and
equipment 23
Wastage from customers' pipes and existing fittings 23
Efficient use by customers 23

Charging for Water Supplies

Charging by volume consumed 26
Metering strategies 27
Tariff structures 28
Tariffs for industrial use 29

Leakage

Expression and significance of leakage 30
Economic levels of leakage 30
Managing leakage 31

Availability of Water Resources and
Security of Supply

The balance between supply and demand 33
Security of supply 33
Funding security of supply 35
Drought orders and permits 35
Drinking water quality 35
Supply failure: compensation 36

Future Need for New Water Resources

Assessment of future needs 37
Influencing future needs 38
Developing use of existing resources 38
Development of new resources 39

Actions 41

References 44

Tables 46

Annex A

Organisations responding to the
invitation to contribute to the
review 54

Annex B

The legal and regulatory framework in respect of water
resources and supply arrangements 55

Annex C

Influencing water demand: some experiences from
other countries 60

Annex D (contributed by the Environment Agency)

Standards of best practice for groundwater yield
assessment 66

Annex E (contributed by the Environment Agency)

Standards of best practice for surface water yield
assessment 70

Annex F (contributed by the Environment Agency)

Standards of best practice for demand analysis and
forecasting 73

Annex G (contributed by the Office of Water Services)

Promoting the efficient use of water by customers . 78

Annex H (contributed by the Office of Water Services)

Metering and tariffs 79

Annex I (contributed by the Office of Water Services)

Leakage assessment and reduction 81

Annex J (contributed by the Office of Water Services)

Continuity and security of supply issues 83

Introduction

In their nature, public water supplies need to be planned on a long-term basis. The continued effectiveness and sufficiency of present arrangements cannot be taken for granted. The requirements of consumers change gradually over time. The impacts of climate change on water resources and on demand for water now need to be taken into account.

This paper considers water resources and supply arrangements in England and Wales. It has been drawn up in discussion with the Office of Water Services, the Environment Agency and representatives of the water companies as the statutory undertakers, and taking into account the comments of a range of other interested bodies. It sets out Ministers' conclusions and the action which they consider ought to be taken by those with the primary responsibility for the particular matter, following the thorough review that has been undertaken.

Water use and sustainable development

The fundamental objectives of water resource and supply systems need to be carefully articulated. Humans make use of water for a wide variety of purposes; some of which are essential for human life and some of which, though not essential, enhance the quality of life. Water is also essential for the rest of natural life, and the character of many eco-systems is determined principally by the particular characteristics of the water environment, whether influenced by human beings or the result of human management. Expectations of public water supplies have developed rapidly over the past two centuries. Demand for household use has been rising gradually, though more modestly in the last two decades. There have been changing expectations for quality and security of supply. Policy needs to reflect these, as well as the possible impact of climate change.

Water is in its nature a renewable resource which, if managed effectively, can be utilised so as to protect eco-systems and allow for multiple reuse. In most circumstances and in most areas in England and Wales, it should be possible to make water available to meet properly managed demand in the foreseeable future in an environmentally responsible manner.

There will usually be costs in protecting the environment and in each case they should be balanced against the benefits that would be achieved. But within the framework of sustainable development,

♦ provided the use of water is rendered sustainable by ensuring that abstraction and subsequent discharge to the environment are appropriately managed so as to protect the environment, and

♦ provided that those who use and discharge the water meet the costs of achieving that protection of the environment (and provided that they meet the costs of collecting, treating, distributing, and taking it away again),

then there is no reason why in most circumstances consumers should not be supplied with the water they want to use beneficially – that is, without waste.

Provided water resources are managed with appropriate protections, there is no environmental virtue in limiting reservoirs and abstractions for their own sake, and the question of providing new resources becomes a matter to be settled with regard to the interests of consumers. Where it is more economical on behalf of the general body of customers,

♦ to manage the use of existing water resources in a more efficient way,

♦ to ensure through the basis of pricing that individual customers or categories of customer meet the true cost of providing the water they use,

♦ to limit leakage from the distribution system and on consumers' own premises,

♦ to encourage or ensure that consumers use water-efficient equipment, and

♦ generally to encourage efficiency in water use by consumers by pricing and in other ways (including possible re-use and recycling by both industry and households),

then the system should seek to ensure that an optimum blend of these measures is in place before moving to the provision of new resources.

It should however be recognised that, even so, there is a possibility that new resources will have to be needed in order to meet growing demand in some areas. Decisions on whether such a need exists should take into account the uncertainties of predicting both demand and the effect of demand management measures; and planning should take into account the long lead-times needed for some new developments. It is now necessary to review water resources and supply plans as expeditiously as possible on a case-by-case basis, taking into account those uncertainties and in particular the effects of climate change on supply and demand, to establish how demand can be managed and met, and

Executive Summary

whether new resources may be needed over the next 25 years.

The legal and regulatory framework

The present framework differs significantly from the centralised, nationalised system which existed up to 1989. It provides for greater flexibility, transparency and clear division of rôles within which the requirements of sustainable development can be addressed. The Government retains the responsibility for ensuring the adequacy of the legal and policy framework within which the water companies and regulators operate, including satisfying itself that arrangements for long term planning of water resources and supply are operating satisfactorily.

In the light of the review the Government considers the basic legal and regulatory framework to be sound. It enables the Government, the three water regulators, and the statutory water undertakers to work together, as appropriate, at national, regional and local levels to ensure that wholesome, sufficient, efficient and well-managed water supplies are available to consumers when they are needed. The Government does not believe that long term planning is best achieved by the creation of a central plan. Further refinement of the framework may, however, be desirable. The Government is considering proposals from the regulators for refinement or extension of their powers and will publish a consultation paper.

Rainfall and climate change

The clustering of droughts over the past 20 years raises important questions concerning both the resilience of existing water supply arrangements and the ability of historic data to provide an appropriate basis for the estimation of yields for existing or new water resource schemes, especially in the light of expected climate change. There is a need to prepare fresh estimates of the current reliable yields of each discrete water resource system, taking into account its current operation and recent hydrometric data.

The Climate Change Impacts Review Group (CCIRG) of the Department of the Environment has recently issued its second report, setting out its best estimate of UK climate change. Against this background, the Government's view is that the fresh estimates of current reliable yields should then be tested against climate change scenarios. The 1996 CCIRG scenario for the United Kingdom and the information which led to its construction should feature prominently in this exercise. Full account should also be taken of further developments in climate change prediction techniques.

Demand for public water supplies

Figures for water put into public supply over the last 20 years show a 15% increase from 1974/5 to 1994/5, but only a 3% increase within the last ten years. There are of course regional variations within these trends, and uncertainties about how immediate past trends, particularly for household use, will continue.

The Government's view is that there is a particular need for water companies to undertake further detailed assessments of how water is used by households in their supply areas in order better to forecast overall demand for water and plan supply in the longer term. Each water company should make its own assessment of overall household use and of the extent to which this varies within its supply area. Each water company should also seek to make an assessment of the micro-components of water use within households in its supply area, taking, where possible, valid account of relevant data from elsewhere. Data should be made publicly available.

Even with better information on present household demand for water, the accuracy of forecasts of future demand will remain heavily dependent on predictions of economic, lifestyle and cultural changes within the community of consumers. Changes in all three of these considerations are likely to be further influenced by climate change. Therefore, it is the Government's view that further studies are needed of the implications of climate change scenarios for demand for public water supplies.

Demand management

It is in the interests of customers to maximise economic beneficial use of existing water resources in order to reduce the need for new resources. It is important to determine and apply the optimum package of demand management measures for each particular water supply system, taking into account the balance between availability of developed resources and the projected changes in demand if no further measures were taken. For all systems, the approach to demand management will blend the common themes of:

- ◆   efficient use,
- ◆   effective and equitable charging arrangements, and
- ◆   economic levels of leakage.

Efficient use

There are three broad areas of activity by which efficiency of water use can be increased:

- provision and installation of more water-efficient equipment and fittings,
- reduction of leakage and other wastage from customers' pipes and existing fittings; and
- promotion of efficient use by customers.

It is essential to regard these activities holistically as offering, in various combinations to suit local circumstances, an effective combined approach to demand management through increased efficiency of water use which, as appropriate, needs to be used in conjunction with price signals to help provide the right framework of incentives.

The Government's view is that renewed effort in these activities would be beneficial, drawing on a range of short- and longer-term options to suit local circumstances and recognising the added incentive for water conservation which volumetric charging provides. Water companies have a statutory duty to promote the efficient use of water by their customers. The Director General of Water Services asked companies to submit their formal strategies for this to him by 1 October 1996.

The Government will bring forward proposals for new water use regulations in the light of advice from its Water Regulations Advisory Committee. The Government looks to manufacturers to continue work to develop water saving equipment, to consumers to co-operate in increasing efficient water use, and to water companies to act individually and collectively to promote water efficiency in all spheres. The Government will explore additional ways in which its Best Practice programmes and other techniques used successfully to implement its environmental management and energy efficiency policies can be used to encourage more efficient use of water.

Charging arrangements

It is for water companies to decide the basis on which they will charge for water supplies. The Government believes however that the gradual extension of metering in combination with the development of more sophisticated tariff structures has an essential rôle to play in managing demand for water and ensuring sustainable water usage against the background of climate change and the growing use of water by households for purposes other than drinking and essential hygiene.

In general, the introduction of metering should be selective, and voluntary in respect of the occupiers who are now charged in their present properties on the basis of rateable values. It also needs to be applied sensitively in respect of those who have high use for essential household purposes. But new properties should continue to be fitted with meters as the norm, as should those which have high external use for garden-watering and swimming pools.

Subject only to the Director General of Water Services' supervision to ensure that pricing is not unduly preferential or discriminatory, water companies are free to tailor their metering strategies to their circumstances using whatever incentives they consider most appropriate in their circumstances. The Government looks to water companies to develop tariff structures which encourage the efficient use of water, and to the regulators to use their powers to encourage that.

Leakage

The Government's view is that, building on existing work, water companies need to:

- apply on a consistent basis methods for estimating and expressing leakage levels;
- assess economic levels of leakage, taking full account of environmental costs; and
- adopt clear programmes and targets for leakage control to economic levels, with rigorous procedures for assessment and reporting of progress in meeting them.

The Director General of Water Services has stated that he expects companies to adopt best practice for leakage economics and to update leakage targets and strategies as appropriate, as part of their demonstration that they are managing their distribution systems in an efficient and prudent manner. If he were to find the targets not defensible by reference to the achievements of comparable companies, he has indicated that he would take this into account in setting price limits, and would also consider enforcement action and the imposition of mandatory targets by the Secretary of State.

Availability of water resources and security of supply

The present situation of water resources for public supply is that England and Wales as a whole are in a posi-

Executive Summary

tion of surplus based on the average demands for water experienced over the last five years. There are quite wide regional variations and some systems may come under significant pressure as demand increases.

The balance point between the availability of water resources and the demand for water to be supplied is defined by the desired security of the water supply system against failure. No uniform standards in respect of security of water supplies currently exist, but one of the clearest lessons from the 1995 drought is that the public generally no longer considers the prospect of standpipes or rota cuts to be tolerable. In principle, security of supply is an aspect of the overall quality of service to the customer and has implications for prices. It is therefore the Government's view that there is a need for greater dialogue between water companies and their customers on the balance to be struck between higher security of supply and higher costs.

This dialogue should start from a fresh estimate and clear communication of the existing capabilities of each discrete water resource and supply system, against the background of maximum economic use of demand management. The dialogue needs to take into account not only the costs of attaining or maintaining a given level of security, but also the more subjective question of consumers' views of the value to them of security of supply. It will assume provision of supplies meeting the required quality standards and will be founded upon recognition of the vital importance of water supplies for public health.

Future need for new water resources

A case for new resources will be compelling only if there is insufficient scope for deployment of existing resources to meet properly-managed demand. In considering this point, companies will naturally look first at options fully within their own control, but should then move on to consider alternatives which would involve actions by others. There is no legal or procedural obstacle to companies making agreements amongst themselves for bulk transfers of water or redistribution of abstraction licences where present organisational boundaries and demand within them do not fully coincide with existing resource availability. The Government believes it is important to ensure that legal and market mechanisms for such processes are effective and that incentives exist to encourage the efficient dis-

tribution of water resources, including the use of price signals where appropriate. It is considering whether these can be improved, and will publish a consultation paper on economic instruments in relation to water abstraction by early 1997.

The Environment Agency has the central rôle in the planning of water resources at the national and regional levels, and is co-ordinating action between water undertakers. However water companies have the duty to develop and maintain an efficient and economical system of water supply within their areas. Compliance with this duty involves them in planning new water resource development where necessary. As the primary responsibility for maintaining water supplies rests with the water companies, so it is the responsibility of those companies, either individually or co-operatively with one another and with full involvement of – or if necessary through enforcement by – the regulators, to draw up plans for the timely development of new resources if the projected demand for water in particular areas cannot be reasonably or reliably managed to remain within the capacity of all the existing resources which could supply those areas.

The costs of new resources, and more generally of effective management of water resources and supply, fall to be considered by the Director General of Water Services within the general financial framework of the industry. This includes a duty on the Director to ensure that water companies can finance their functions. Whether a particular scheme calls for an increase in revenue will depend on the overall financial position and efficiency of the company as assessed by the Director.

In considering the nature and timing of new developments, significant allowance has to be made for the planning process, which is likely to be protracted in view of the imperative to consider carefully the environmental impact of any new scheme, and the margin of uncertainty in the particular case. Moreover, there has to be a clear strategy for maintaining supplies in the meantime at an acceptable level of security. The Government's view is that planning of new resource development for areas where the existing resources are most finely balanced against projected demand increases should proceed in parallel with the continued implementation of measures to meet that demand from already-developed resources, and against the background of a continuous review of that balance.

Actions

The Government will:

♦ bring forward modifications to the legal framework if scope for further refinement were to. emerge (although it is satisfied that the basic framework is sound);

♦ continue to promote research into climate change;

♦ revise regulatory requirements in respect of water conservation in the light of advice from its Water Regulations Advisory Committee;

♦ review the process for Drought Order applications;

♦ draw on its experience in promoting environmental management and energy efficiency to assist the relevant organisations in the promotion of efficient use of water;

♦ introduce legislation as necessary for compensation arrangements for customers affected by supply interruptions or low pressure; and

♦ consult on the use of economic instruments in relation to water abstraction.

The **Environment Agency** should:

♦ co-ordinate the fresh estimating of the reliable yields of water resource systems and publish the resulting information;

♦ lead the testing of those estimates against climate change scenarios;

♦ revise as necessary its national and regional water resources strategies in consultation with the water companies; and

♦ be fully involved with water companies' new resource development plans.

The **Office of Water Services** should:

♦ monitor and as necessary enforce water companies' performance of their duty to promote the efficient use of water by their customers;

♦ monitor, report and, as necessary, take further action on leakage control;

♦ be fully involved with water companies' new resource development plans; and

♦ consider the financial implications of new water resources and supply schemes as necessary in the course of its normal price regulation activities.

The **Drinking Water Inspectorate** will:

♦ check that all water supplies are monitored in accordance with and meet regulatory quality requirements;

♦ check that water treatment processes comply with regulatory requirements; and

♦ take enforcement action if regulatory requirements are not met.

Water companies should:

♦ prepare fresh estimates of the reliable yields of water resource systems;

♦ establish further detailed measurements of household water use;

♦ conduct further studies of the implications of climate change on demand for water;

♦ extend the penetration of metering;

♦ develop more sophisticated tariff structures;

♦ increase efforts to promote water conservation;

♦ improve leakage measurement, control and reporting;

♦ enter into dialogue with customers about security of supply; and

♦ draw up plans for timely development of new water resources where demand cannot be managed to remain within existing resource capability.

Manufacturers of water-using equipment and fittings should:

♦ continue to develop and market energetically more water-efficient products; and

♦ continue innovation in the field of water recycling systems.

Water consumers should:

♦ take full notice of information from water companies and other organisations on the need for water efficiency and how to achieve it;

♦ recognise the environmental significance of water conservation; and

♦ take every opportunity to use water wisely.

It is the regulators' duty to ensure that water companies are carrying out their tasks properly. It is for the Government to ensure that the legal and regulatory framework is in good order and to give policy guidance as appropriate on use of regulatory powers. This paper provides broad policy and strategic guidance.

Consumers have an important contribution to make towards the management and use of water resources in the wider public interest. Nevertheless, many of the actions identified in this paper fall to the water companies. This is as it should be; they should have the knowledge, skills, customer awareness and financial resources with which to give effect to their duty as water undertakers to maintain public water supplies both now and in the longer term.

Introduction

1.1 On 1 September 1995, the Secretary of State for the Environment announced that he had asked officials, in consultation with the Office of Water Services, the National Rivers Authority (as it then was), the Drinking Water Inspectorate, the Water Services Association and the Water Companies Association, and other interested organisations, to conduct a review of the lessons of the developing drought for water resources and supply arrangements in the longer term. An outline programme of work was drawn up. Contributions in its terms were subsequently invited by letter to 77 other organisations likely to have an interest in the matter and 22 responses have been received. Annex A lists the organisations that responded. Copies of their comments can be consulted in the Department of the Environment library.

1.2 More recently, the review process has taken account of the early discussions of the Water Sub-Group of the Round Table on Sustainable Development, and also published memoranda of evidence to the Inquiry into Water Conservation and Supply which the Environment Committee of the House of Commons began in May 1996.

1.3 This paper has been drawn up in discussion with the Office of Water Services, the Environment Agency, the Drinking Water Inspectorate and representatives of the water companies as the statutory undertakers. It considers water resources and supply arrangements only in England and Wales[3]. It sets out Ministers' conclusions and the action which they consider ought to be taken by those with the primary responsibility for the particular matter, whether the Government itself, Parliament, the Director General of Water Services, the Environment Agency (the successor to the National Rivers Authority), the water undertakers, water equipment manufacturers, or water consumers.

1.4 The paper focuses on the question of public water supplies – those provided to consumers of all kinds by the statutory water undertakers, whether for domestic purposes (to which the statutory duties of the undertakers relate)[4] or for other purposes such as use in industrial processes. It does not deal with private supplies[5], including those for industrial purposes, or the abstraction of water for agricultural purposes, which is significant in some of the drier eastern areas of the country. The resources available for public supply purposes may however be affected by these other uses, and where necessary the Environment Agency must seek to achieve a proper balance between the different needs in exercising its duty of taking all such action as it may from time to time consider to be necessary and expedient for the purpose of conserving, redistributing or otherwise augmenting water resources and securing their proper use[6].

1.5 The paper examines the overall policy and strategy which it is necessary to pursue in order to maintain sufficient and efficient public water supplies over the next few decades.

1.6 This engages a considerable number of closely linked, interactive factors – rainfall, the yield of existing resources, changing patterns of demand, the efficiency and economy of the distribution system, efficiency and economy of use by customers, and the price signals which affect patterns of use. All these matters affect the question of whether existing systems are capable of providing sufficient water to meet both average and peak demand from consumers in all circumstances in the longer term. The whole needs to be viewed against the background of the need for policies and strategies which are consistent with the principle of sustainable development, and which take account of the likely effects of climate change in England and Wales at regional and local levels over the next few decades.

1.7 The paper therefore looks first at the **overall context of water use and sustainable development**, before assessing the **effectiveness of the current legal and regulatory framework** for the overall management of water resource and supply matters. It then turns to a consideration of **rainfall and water re-**

---

3   The situations in Scotland and Northern Ireland are somewhat different, particularly in respect of the organisation of the water industry.

4   Statutorily, water supplied for domestic purposes is that supplied for drinking, washing, cooking, central heating and sanitary purposes (excluding water used in laundries, or for food or drink preparation if the food or drink is consumed off the premises), irrespective of whether the user is a domestic, industrial or commercial customer. While undertakers are obliged, on request, to supply water for domestic purposes, their responsibility to supply water for other purposes is different. Further details are given in Annex B.

5   Private supplies are made under contractual arrangements between the supplier and the consumer, and the supplier has no statutory duty of supply though if the water is used for drinking it must meet the statutory requirements of the Private Water Supplies Regulations 1991, which incorporate the requirements of the European Community "Drinking Water" Directive of 1980.

6   Section 6(2) of the Environment Act 1995.

source yields and of the possible effects on them of climate change before going on to look at aspects of the demand for public water supplies – its measurement and its possible future evolution. The next three sections of the paper each consider broad ways in which demand for water supplies can be managed – through price signals, by increasing efficiency of use and by control of leakage – although, as the paper makes clear, these three ways should be applied together in an appropriate mix in each case in order to provide optimum management of demand in different circumstances.

1.8   In the light of this analysis, the paper looks at the likely balance between availability of water resources and demand in the longer term and considers the issue of security of supply which in part defines that balance. It then concludes by looking in the light of the preceding conclusions at the issue of the development of new water resources.

1.9   Of the annexes, Annexes A, B and C provide additional information in support of the main text. So do Annexes D to J, but they set out what their originators (the Office of Water Services or the Environment Agency, as shown at the head of each page) consider to represent present good practice in respect of the topics addressed. The material in each of these is open to further consultation and development amongst the relevant organisations – a process which should be encouraged by consideration of the material set out in the main paper. Comments on these annexes, to be sent to the relevant originator, are invited by the date shown in their introductory paragraphs.

1.10   In general, the paper looks at the subject from the perspective of England and Wales as a whole. Most of the quantitative information is given on that basis. However, it is essential to bear in mind that the situation with respect to water resources and supplies varies widely both between and within regions. Because of these variations, the strategy and management of water resources and supply systems need to be on a case-by-case basis: uniform national solutions are likely to be inappropriate. The paper sets out a policy framework and agenda for action within which such case-by-case consideration can proceed.

The Overall Context: Water Use and Sustainable Development

2.1   Any review of water resources and supply in the longer term needs to begin by asking questions about the fundamental objectives to be achieved by water supply systems in a world in which any human use of water must be sustainable in the longer term. These basic objectives need to be carefully articulated or there will be a danger that policies and strategies for water supply will be founded on a false basis.

2.2   As physical beings, humans in the modern world make use of water for a wide variety of purposes, for example, for drinking, for hygiene and sanitation, for a wide range of agricultural and industrial purposes, to enhance amenity whether through artificial lakes and fountains or to water public and private gardens, and for a range of leisure purposes like swimming, canoeing, boating and fishing. Some of these uses are essential for human life. Others enhance the quality of life and are none the less desirable for that – increasingly, we expect to be able to benefit from these sorts of uses.

2.3   Water is essential for the rest of natural life as well, and the character of many ecosystems is determined principally by the particular characteristics of their water environment, whether uninfluenced by human beings or the result of beneficial human management[7]. Few human activities have no influence on the water environment, and sometimes human needs and those of the rest of the particular ecosystem or systems concerned may conflict in a manner which demands particularly careful management with associated costs. In some cases there can be irresolvable conflicts which involve difficult choices with implications for one or other set of needs.

2.4   Expectations of public water supplies have developed rapidly over the last two centuries. Initially they were enjoyed only by the well-to-do in urban areas. Now 99% of the population of the UK have such supplies, as do virtually all business premises. Originally, supply was confined to a few hours each day[8]; from the end of the nineteenth century, continuous supply became the norm, for cost and efficiency reasons as well as for the benefits to consumers. Changes in hygiene practices and the introduction of labour-saving equipment such as automatic washing machines and dishwashers have increased demand for water use over the last half century – a trend which has been partly offset by the use of equipment which uses less water, although there is concern that increases in the number of single-person households and the plausible consequent further increases in the use of such equipment may reduce the overall impact of its water-use efficiency. There has been a reduction in industrial demand as a result of changes in industrial structure and of more efficient use of water by industry encouraged by the extension of volumetric payment. Lately, there has been renewed concern that demand for garden watering is increasing rapidly.

2.5   These changes have been reflected in gradually rising demand for household use. Whereas in 1961 usage per head was 85 litres per day, usage now stands at about 150 litres per day. Growth of use for this purpose has been more modest in the last two decades than in the 1960s (about 1.4% per annum as against 2.7%). But water use does need to be viewed in the light of the fact that, leaving aside the effects of countervailing factors such as the use of more water-efficient equipment and price pressures, the desire to use water as a commodity for all purposes is likely to rise with rising wealth and related social changes[9]. Climate change leading to greater variability of rainfall and higher tem-

---

7   In this context, it is worth noting that, in the United Kingdom, many valuable water environments as well as valuable landscapes are the product of human management over the centuries. Some are almost entirely natural; some are the accidental by-product of human activity and subsequent management (for example, the Broads and the West Yorkshire rivers); and some like the Somerset levels and the Thames virtually throughout its freshwater length are the product of positive human management which must be maintained if the present appearance and ecology are to be sustained.

8   That explains the use of cisterns in individual premises in the UK system. The purpose was to provide a supply during the hours when the public supply was not available.

9   Use by households, in litres/head/day and including outdoor use was, in (year):

United Kingdom	149	(1994/95)	Netherlands	171	(1993)
Germany	132	(1995)	France	157	(1993)
Japan	250-300	(1996)	USA	473	(1996)
USA (excluding outdoor)	284	(1996)			

The variations in these figures are probably attributable to a variety of factors. It is clear that they are heavily influenced by differences in climate (even within, for example, the USA) and traditions in equipment and usage, and there is no need to expect consumption levels in Europe rapidly to approach US or Japanese levels. In the USA major efforts of demand-side management, particularly through the price mechanism, are being made to reduce consumption per capita. Further information is contained in Annex C.

peratures may also lead to increased demand for use by households.

2.6 Policy on water resources and water supply needs to take these points into account. The wish of human beings to use water for a wide variety of purposes should not be regarded as an evil in itself – which is not to say its use should not be properly managed so as, for example, to increase the efficiency of use, minimise waste and unnecessary costs, and to protect the environment.

2.7 Policy also needs to take note of changing public attitudes towards means of managing supplies in times of relatively low rainfall. Historically, systems of water supply in the United Kingdom have been designed on the assumption that in such periods supply and demand would be balanced by means of administrative rationing. For many years, the legislation has therefore allowed for hosepipe bans, bans on non-essential use, and interruptions of supply in cases of shortage of rainfall. It is frequently said that water resource and supply systems in this country have been designed on the assumption that hosepipe bans would have to be applied every 10 years or so, that restrictions on non-essential uses might have to be introduced less frequently, and that there might have to be resort to standpipes and/or rota cuts every 50 – 100 years. However, this has never been more than a matter of custom and practice, and the evidence is that very many systems are in fact more robust than that.

2.8 As is frequently the case however when society becomes accustomed to depending on a particular engineering system, customers now assume that there will be a continuous, unlimited supply of water. Hospitals and residential care facilities, and the care of those with special needs, such as dialysis patients, would be hopelessly disrupted by interruptions for which satisfactory alternative arrangements could not be made. The economic and social effects of interruptions to industrial and commercial supply are also highly undesirable, if not completely unsustainable. It is apparent from recent events that society does not consider it tolerable to design water supply systems on the basis that reductions or interruptions of service will be necessary from time to time, though it may be questionable whether society has faced up to the cost implications of guaranteeing practically unlimited supplies in all circumstances. (It is possible that consumers may still accept hosepipe bans as a reasonable rationing measure in dry weather, but that may depend on their percep-

tion of the particular circumstances of the case, and it is an issue on which attitudes might change with changing approaches to garden maintenance.)

2.9 This leads to the question whether it is sustainable in environmental terms to meet an increasing demand for water in all circumstances.

2.10 First, it should noted that water is in its nature a renewable rather than an unrenewable resource. Once used for water supply, it is returned to a water body or finds its way to an aquifer. Even that which evaporates returns to liquid form in due course, and more generally the water cycle ultimately returns water for possible re-use. Provided that water is not polluted with long-lasting and bio-accumulating substances, it is not in the long term damaged by its use; and shorter term impacts (of, for example, nutrients and temperature) can also be managed to the extent that is necessary to prevent degradation of the receiving environment. So long as arrangements are in place to manage abstraction and discharge effectively on a river basin basis, downstream eco-systems can be protected and multiple re-use is feasible, as has long been the case in, for example, the Thames basin.

2.11 On the other hand, abstraction from surface water and aquifers can in some cases have unacceptable impact on water levels and the dependent ecological systems. New reservoirs in specific locations may have an unacceptable impact in environmental and/or social terms (although they can be designed in ways that give both enhanced habitat for wildlife[10] and a variety of new leisure opportunities, not only on and around the reservoir itself, but also as a result of augmenting the natural level of river flow downstream). But it will frequently be possible to avoid these impacts by abstracting from elsewhere in the neighbourhood, or by bringing water by river transfer or pipeline a shorter or longer distance (taking into account of course any environmental impact of the possibly different characteristics of the incoming water).

2.12 In most circumstances and in most areas in England and Wales, it should be possible to make water available by some means or other to meet properly-managed demand for public water supplies in the foreseeable future in an environmentally-responsible manner. This is likely to be so, even taking possible climate change into account – though further research

---

10   The Government is committed by various means, including international conventions and EC directives, to the conservation of biodiversity of species and habitats, as stated in its response (published in May 1996) to the December 1995 report of the United Kingdom Biodiversity Steering Group.

and analysis is necessary as a matter of urgency to verify that that is so.

2.13 There will usually be costs, of course, of protecting the environment and in each case they should be balanced against the benefits that would be achieved. But within the framework of sustainable development,

- provided the use of water is rendered sustainable by ensuring that abstraction and subsequent discharge to the environment are appropriately managed so as to protect the environment, and
- provided that those who use and discharge the water meet the costs of achieving that protection of the environment (and provided that they meet the costs of collecting, treating, distributing, and taking it away again),

then there is no reason why in most circumstances consumers should not be supplied with the water they want to use beneficially – that is, without waste[11].

2.14 This is a general statement, and it should be noted that, if it is necessary in particular cases to provide new resources to meet well-managed demand, it may not be possible to do so without incurring higher than average costs – with implications for prices to the customers who would benefit. In addition, in certain areas there may be periods of real scarcity of water resources in relation to demand upon them. That may demand some mechanism for allocating the scarce resource, including perhaps the use of an economic instrument relating to abstraction – a subject on which the Department of the Environment is preparing a separate paper. Such an instrument might include incentive charges going beyond the costs of abstraction, treatment and distribution as one mechanism for containing pressures on scarce resources and allocating them between potential consumers.

2.15 So long as action is taken on the lines of paragraphs 2.9 to 2.13 are met, there is no environmental virtue in limiting reservoirs and abstractions for their own sake, and the question of providing new resources becomes a matter to be settled with regard to the interests of consumers. If it is more economical on behalf of the general body of customers,

- to manage the use of existing water resources in a more efficient way,

- to ensure through the basis of pricing that individual customers or categories of customer meet the true cost of providing the water they use,
- to limit leakage from the distribution system and on customers' own premises,
- to encourage or ensure that consumers use water-efficient equipment, and
- generally to encourage efficiency in water use by consumers by pricing and in other ways (including possible re-use and recycling by both industry and households),

then the system should seek to ensure that these measures are in place before moving to the provision of new resources. It is of course necessary to achieve the optimum blend of these demand management measures and not to concentrate on one, such as leakage, while neglecting the others.

2.16 It should however be recognised that, even with the application of the measures outlined in paragraph 2.15, there is a possibility that new resources will have to be provided in order to meet growing demand in some areas. Decisions on whether such a need exists should take into account the uncertainties of predicting both demand and the effect of demand management measures. The decisions must also take account of the long lead-times likely to be needed to develop new water resources. If a new resource is needed it becomes necessary to find an environmentally-sustainable solution, consistent with the criteria outlined in paragraphs 2.9 to 2.13. In any particular case, it is likely to be necessary for the Environment Agency (or the Secretary of State on appeal), in determining the application for the new abstraction or impoundment licence, to make a judgment as to the relative costs and benefits of alternative solutions. It will be necessary also for the Director General of Water Services to make a judgment as to the extent of security of supply for which customers are prepared to pay.

2.17 It is within this general framework of sustainable development as it applies to public water supplies that each component of the water resources and supply system is considered below.

---

11   An analogous argument also applies to the question of whether development should be refused in a particular location or locations on grounds of water supply difficulties. If the developer can arrange for the supply of water in an environmentally-acceptable manner, water supply should not in itself be a reason for refusing planning permission, though a particular development may of course be unacceptable for other reasons.

The Legal and Regulatory Framework

Preamble

3.1 Since the onset of the present drought in the spring of 1995, much has been done by the water companies, in consultation with their regulators, to reinforce, and improve the efficiency of, water resources and supply systems where necessary. It has become clear, however, that it would be helpful to clarify for Parliament and the public where the different responsibilities for water resources and water supplies now lie. The arrangements differ fundamentally from those under the centralised, nationalised system up to 1989 and, in **the Government's view**, are as a result much more satisfactory and effective for the current purposes. Greater public understanding of the framework is one purpose of the detail provided in this section of the paper and the related Annex B.

3.2 The present legal and regulatory framework for the water industry in England and Wales was erected mainly by the Water Act 1989 and subsequently consolidated into the Water Industry Act 1991 and the Water Resources Act 1991. Some modifications and additions to this framework were made in the Environment Act 1995 and in the Competition and Service (Utilities) Act 1992, but the concept and structure of the 1989 framework has remained substantially unaltered.

3.3 The Secretary of State is responsible for this framework. He appoints three regulators for the industry. The **Director General of Water Services** is appointed under section 1 of the Water Industry Act 1991 and has the key duty to secure that the functions of a water undertaker are properly financed and carried out. The **Environment Agency** is a body corporate, with members appointed by Ministers under section 1 of the Environment Act 1995. In respect of water resources, the Agency has the key duty to conserve, redistribute or otherwise augment water resources in England and Wales and to secure the proper use of those resources. Further detail on the general function of these two regulators is given in Annex B. The **Drinking Water Inspectorate** embodies the powers of the Secretary of State under section 86 of the Water Industry Act 1991 to appoint assessors for the enforcement of water quality.

3.4 The legal framework in respect of water resources and supply arrangements comprises several components which are described in more detail in Annex B. In order to set the scene for what follows in the main body of this paper, some key components are discussed in the remainder of this section.

Duty to maintain water supply

3.5 The statutory responsibility for public water supplies rests with companies which are appointed as water undertakers under section 6 of the Water Industry Act 1991. Under section 37 of that Act, a water undertaker has the duty:

'to develop and maintain an efficient and economical system of water supply within its area and to ensure that all such arrangements have been made…

(a)   for providing supplies of water to premises in that area and for making such supplies available to persons who demand them; and

(b)   for maintaining, improving and extending the water undertaker's water mains and other pipes,

as are necessary for securing that the undertaker is and continues to be able to meet its obligations'
under Part III of the Act on water supply.

3.6 The terms of this duty are such as to require water companies to plan in an effective manner to provide water supplies in their areas in the future.

3.7 Prudently managed water companies can be expected to carry out this duty in a competent manner, but it is enforceable, under section 18 of the Water Industry Act 1991, by the Secretary of State or the Director General of Water Services. Enforcement provides a mechanism whereby the Secretary of State or Director can specify the action to be taken by a company which is in breach of any enforceable duty. If enforcement action is initiated, provision is made under section 19 of the Act for the company to offer a legally-binding undertaking to carry out specific steps to remedy the breach within a deadline. If the undertaking is accepted by the enforcing authority, there is no need to move to an enforcement order so long as the steps and deadline given in the undertaking are honoured and remain acceptable.

3.8 The Water Industry Act 1991 distinguishes between supplies for domestic and non-domestic purposes. The meaning of "domestic purposes" in relation to water supply is defined in section 218 of that Act as water used for drinking, washing, cooking, central heating or sanitary purposes. Domestic purposes also includes those outside the house (including the washing of vehicles and the watering of gardens) which are connected with the occupation of the house and which may be satisfied by water drawn from a tap inside the house and without the use of a hosepipe or similar apparatus.

3.9 Where supplies are requested for other than domestic purposes, it is the duty of water undertaker for the area under section 55(2) of the Act to provide that supply. However, a water undertaker is under no obligation to provide a new supply to any premises for non-domestic purposes if that provision would put at risk the water undertaker's ability to meet its existing obligations in respect of water supply for all purposes or its ability to meet likely future demands for domestic supplies.

Quality of water supplies

3.10 Under section 68 of the Water Industry Act 1991, water undertakers, when supplying water to any premises for domestic or food production purposes, have the duty to supply only water which is wholesome at the time of supply. Water is regarded as wholesome if the requirements set out in regulation 3 of the Water Supply (Water Quality) Regulations 1989 (as amended in 1989 and 1991) are met. This is a duty enforceable by the Secretary of State under section 18 of the Water Industry Act 1991. The Secretary of State may also prosecute water undertakers for the offence of supplying water unfit for human consumption under section 70 of the Act. Technical assessment of drinking water quality and advice to the Secretary of State on enforcement action or on prosecution is provided by the Drinking Water Inspectorate.

Water use

3.11 The Environment Act 1995 has given every water undertaker the duty to promote the efficient use of water by its customers, enforceable by the Secretary of State or the Director General of Water Services. The duty is one of promotion; under section 93A(3) water undertakers are explicitly barred from imposing any requirement on their customers or potential customers. However, the Director has the power to require water undertakers to take specific action or to achieve specific overall standards of performance in respect of this duty.

3.12 Contamination, wastage or undue consumption of water by or through fittings which are the responsibility of the customer constitutes an offence under section 73 of the Water Industry Act 1991. Section 74 of the Act empowers the Secretary of State to make regulations for preventing contamination or waste from

water fittings. Such regulations will replace the existing Water Byelaws (see paragraph 7.10 ff).

Water resource management

3.13 Under section 6(2) of the Environment Act 1995, the Environment Agency has the duty
'*to take all such action as it may from time to time consider... ...to be necessary or expedient for the purpose-*
(a)   *of conserving, redistributing or otherwise augmenting water resources in England and Wales; and*
(b)   *of securing the proper use of water resources in England and Wales.*'

3.14 This duty gives the Environment Agency the central rôle in the planning of water resources at the national and regional levels, and in co-ordinating action between water undertakers. Section 6(2) goes on to say that this duty on the Agency does not relieve any water undertaker of its obligation to develop water resources for the purpose of performing its duties under section 37 of the Water Industry Act 1991. These provisions have the effect of making it necessary for the Environment Agency and water companies to work together in water resource development. Section 11 of this paper discusses this arrangement in more detail.

3.15 To the extent that it considers appropriate for carrying out these duties, the Environment Agency has, under section 20(1) of the Water Resources Act 1991, a duty, so far as is reasonably practicable, to enter into and maintain arrangements with water undertakers for securing the proper management or operation of water resources available for their use and of any reservoirs, apparatus or other works under their control. Obligations upon water undertakers under such arrangements are enforceable by the Secretary of State under section 18 of the Water Industry Act 1991.

Environmental duties

3.16 The Secretary of State, the Director General of Water Services and every company holding appointment as a water undertaker each have a duty, under section 3 of the Water Industry Act 1991, to consider the natural and built environment when formulating or considering any proposals relating to the functions of an undertaker. Obligations of water undertakers which result from these provisions are enforceable by the Secretary of State under section 18 of the Act.

3.17 Ministers and the Environment Agency have, under sections 7 and 8 of the Environment Act 1995, similar wide ranging duties in respect of formulating or considering proposals relevant to the functions of water undertakers. The Environment Agency has, under section 6(1) of that Act, duties generally to promote environmental and recreational considerations with respect to water. Under section 4 of the Act, it has as its principal aim contribution towards the attainment of the objective of achieving sustainable development.

Summary

3.18 The components outlined above, taken with the others described in Annex B, combine in a legal framework which:

(a) places operational responsibility in respect of the sufficiency and quality of public water supplies squarely on water companies;

(b) requires the Director General of Water Services to secure that prudent and well-managed water companies are able to finance the proper carrying out of their functions;

(c) assigns the Environment Agency, subject to a specific power of direction from the Secretary of State which he would expect to use only in the last resort, the rôle of strategic planning and management of water resources, while maintaining an obligation on water companies to develop water resources;

(d) empowers the regulators to obtain information in order to assess water companies' performance of their duties;

(e) provides for enforcement action to compel companies to deal with any breaches of their duties;

(f) provides for secondary legislation if necessary for the further articulation of companies' duties or the prevention of contamination and waste;

(g) empowers Ministers to give directions to companies or regulators and to decide appeals in particular classes of case; and

(h) requires Government, regulators and the water companies alike to enhance the natural environment through their actions and otherwise to have full regard for the environmental effects of their actions in maintaining and developing water resources and supplies.

3.19 The scope and adaptability of this framework provide many mechanisms by which water resource and supply arrangements are consolidated and improved. Companies and regulators alike need to keep in view the ways in which these mechanisms may be combined to maintain for the public the excellent standards of service which it is their common aim to secure while protecting the environment. There is no fundamental legal constraint within the framework set up by the 1991 Acts to the achievement of that aim.

3.20 **The Government's view** is that the basic legal and regulatory framework for making decisions concerning water resources and supply arrangements in the longer term is sound. The framework enables the Government, the three water regulators, and the statutory water undertakers to work together, as appropriate, at national, regional and local levels to ensure that wholesome, sufficient, efficient and well-managed water supplies are available to consumers when they are needed.

3.21 So far as the overall process of strategic planning for water resources in the longer term at the national and regional levels is concerned, the lead lies with the Environment Agency, but the Agency must proceed in the closest consultation with water companies, since it is they who have the front-line duty of ensuring that their customers' needs for water are met and it is they who, individually or jointly, must assemble the investment resources for any major schemes that may be needed. There is further discussion of this matter in Section 11 of this paper.

3.22 What follows in this paper is, in effect, a review of the policy and strategic situation with respect to water resources and supply in the longer term at the national level, as it appears in the summer of 1996. This review has been conducted through consultation and discussion within the framework described above.

Amendment of the legal framework

3.23 In July 1996, the Environment Agency and the Director General of Water Services separately indicated to Government and to the Environment Committee of the House of Commons (see paragraph 1.2) that there are a few issues concerning the powers and duties of each regulator which should be addressed in order to establish whether the range of mechanisms could usefully be refined or extended to enhance the ability of each to discharge its responsibilities as efficiently and effectively as possible within the basic framework described above. **The Government is considering these proposals** with the regulators concerned and has made it clear that any necessary changes will be pursued. A consultation paper will be published in due course.

Rainfall and Climate Change

Droughts

4.1 The droughts of 1995/96, 1988-92, 1984 and 1975/76 may be considered as exceptionally rare events for specific time spans and for specific parts of England and Wales. For each the rainfall deficiency was of sufficient magnitude and duration to affect water resources over wide areas, and to test severely the ability of water supply systems to satisfy demands. Each has its own hydrological and consequential characteristics – as discussed in a recent paper (Marsh and Turton, 1996) there is no single type of drought although some broad categorisation may be made.

4.2 The clustering of droughts over the past 20 years raises important questions concerning both the resilience of existing water supply arrangements and the ability of historic data to provide an appropriate basis for the estimation of yields for existing or new water resource schemes. There is a need to address the question of whether severe droughts such as that of 1995/96 are occurring more often, whether climate data show any trends, and if so whether the yield or management of water supply systems should be revised.

4.3 In general, only those droughts that persist for at least four or five months will cause significant stress to water resource systems, and then only the smaller storages would be greatly affected. Larger storages such as major reservoirs and groundwater are most depleted by droughts that persist for at least two summers and an intervening winter.

4.4 The 1995 drought was exceptionally severe over the five months from April to August 1995, being the driest five month period since 1850, as shown in Table 1. It should be noted that the two most severe five month events occurred in the last 20 years. The dry conditions have persisted into 1996; by the end of August only three months since April 1995 had produced above average rainfall for England and Wales as a whole. Only in the drought of 1975/76 has there been a lower 17-month rainfall total (for any start month in the 228 years covered by records) than that for April 1995 to August 1996.

Rainfall and water resource yields

4.5 Average monthly and annual rainfall data are important parameters for the design of water resource schemes. However these data have changed over the years because the standard 30 or 35 year periods have been successively updated. Table 2 shows the mean monthly and annual data for England and Wales for three standard periods, 1916-50, 1941-70 and 1961-90, each of which has been used for planning and estimating the yield of various water resource systems. An examination of these data showed that rainfall has tended to increase in March and decrease in July and August. Clearly, it is now prudent to incorporate the most recent rainfall data in the estimation of water resource yields.

4.6 Reliable yields of existing and possible future water resources are estimated from rainfall and other hydrological data sets which may be of various lengths, sometimes incomplete and characterised by varying standards of accuracy. Estimates also necessarily take account of the physical characteristics and constraints of the natural and built components which define the water resource.

4.7 Changes may have occurred in the nature or configuration of some resources. For example, some surface water sources which were originally developed independently have subsequently been incorporated into "conjunctive use" schemes in which several sources, perhaps spread over a relatively wide geographic area encompassing more than one river catchment, provide an aggregated water resource for a large supply area and which are managed accordingly. The run-off which feeds surface water sources may also have been changed in its volume or distribution as a result of changing catchment characteristics such as the extent of afforestation. Ground water resources, although generally less susceptible to changes in potential yields, may be subject to variation in their actual yields if aquifer contamination (for example, by saline intrusion) renders the resource unsuitable in water quality terms.

4.8 There appears to be no substantial body of information on the extent to which re-assessment of reliable yields in the light of these considerations might result in changes to the estimated overall resource position. There has been no single method of estimating reliable yields to which all water companies and the Environment Agency subscribe, although the National Rivers Authority (NRA) commissioned a research report (NRA, 1995a) on the matter which is now providing the basis for a common approach under the auspices of the Environment Agency. Annexes D and E set out the Agency's views on standards of best practice in assessing the yield respectively of groundwater and surface water resources.

4.9 The Government's view is that there is a need to prepare – by means of up to date consistent assumptions and methodology – fresh estimates of the current reliable yields of each discrete water resource system, taking into account its current operation and recent hydrometric data.

4.10 This action needs to be taken urgently by all water companies. It is clearly desirable for this process to be extended to all water resource systems so as to enable regional and local water resources and supply strategies to be reviewed and revised as necessary. The Environment Agency should co-ordinate the process and collate the resulting information. The Government would wish this information to be published by the Agency by the end of 1997.

Climate change

4.11 The effects of climate change may become increasingly significant on rainfall patterns and hence on water resource availability. The Intergovernmental Panel on Climate Change (IPCC) – set up jointly by the World Meteorological Organization and the United Nations Environment Programme – has recently produced (IPCC, 1996) a "Summary for Policymakers" which states that global climate has changed over the past century and is expected to continue to change in the future. The report states that `the balance of evidence suggests a discernible human influence on global climate'. It points out that greenhouse gas concentrations have increased over the past century, leading to a warming of the Earth's surface which is consistent with model calculations when the local cooling influence of anthropogenic aerosols is also taken into account.

4.12 The IPCC points out that many factors currently limit its ability to project and detect future climate change. Nevertheless, it has developed a range of six scenarios of future greenhouse gas and aerosol precursor emissions based on assumptions about changes in the various contributory factors. The scenarios lead to projected increases in global mean surface air temperature relative to that in 1990 of between 1°C and 3.5°C by the year 2100, with a best estimate of 2°C.

4.13 The Climate Change Impacts Review Group (CCIRG) of the Department of the Environment has recently issued its second report (CCIRG, 1996). This sets out the Group's best estimate of UK climate change, but the CCIRG points out that it describes only one possible future evolution of climate

and that it is impossible to attribute a probability to any one scenario. The CCIRG 1996 scenario explicitly does not include the effects of aerosols on future climate.

4.14 In the CCIRG scenario, UK temperatures are expected to rise at about 0.2°C per decade, with slightly slower rates over the North West than the South East. Extremely warm seasons and years are expected to occur more frequently, with a hot summer such as that in 1995 likely to be a 1-in-3 year event by the sixth decade of the next century rather than the 1-in-90 event as which it is currently regarded.

4.15 Under the CCIRG scenario:
(a) annual precipitation over the UK as a whole will increase by about 5% from its present level by the third decade of the next century;
(b) winter precipitation will increase everywhere, but more substantially over the southern part of the country;
(c) summer precipitation will decrease over the South, but will increase over the North;
(d) evaporative losses of rainfall will be increased at all times of the year throughout England and Wales, with a consequent reduction in the effective rainfall which in turn determines the extent of run-off and availability of surface water resources;
(e) there would however be a general increase in river flow in winter but a decrease, especially in the South, during summer, with consequences for the seasonal availability of surface water for abstraction for public water supply; and
(f) despite heavier winter rainfall, ground water recharge may be reduced because higher evaporative loss and longer-lasting soil moisture deficits in the autumn and early winter would curtail the recharge season.

4.16 This CCIRG report points out that no published studies of water resources have yet used this scenario. However, some simulations were conducted by the CCIRG for its review and the report goes on to outline the implications for river and groundwater abstraction and reservoir storage. Earlier work demonstrated the quite widely differing consequences for that aspect of water resources which would result from different scenarios and was summarised in a subsequent publication (Parry and Duncan, 1995).

4.17 Against this background, the Government's view is that the fresh estimates of current reliable yields which it would wish to be made urgently (see

Rainfall and Climate Change

paragraph 4.9f) should then be tested against climate change scenarios. The 1996 CCIRG scenario for the United Kingdom and the information which led to its construction should feature prominently in this exercise. Full account should also be taken of further developments in climate change prediction techniques, together with the more recent scenarios available from the Hadley Centre. This work should be done as part of the analysis which will need to underlie the review and revision of regional and local water resources and supply strategies. As climate prediction techniques continue to be developed, these should be taken into account in further studies.

4.18 Particularly with the recent CCIRG work now to hand, there is sufficient information available for an immediate start to be made on this process. The Government would expect the Environment Agency to take the lead, in full consultation with the water companies and the Global Atmosphere Division of the Department of the Environment, and necessarily in close contact with centres of excellence on climate change studies. The Global Atmosphere Division runs, as part of the Department's Environmental Protection re-

search programme, the Climate Prediction Programme (CPP), which is carried out by the Hadley Centre for Climate Prediction and Research at the Meteorological Office. The CPP has informed the work of the CCIRG and further scenarios are being prepared as models are developed further. The development of high resolution regional models may help improve the prediction of rainfall over smaller regions such the British Isles.

4.19 It will be important to construct from the tests a range of consequences for water resource yields. Through the scenario-based previous work of the NRA on water resources (see paragraph 10.3ff), the Environment Agency will be no stranger to this approach.

4.20 The output from this work will be needed to inform consideration of the future availability and security of water supplies (see section 10) and the possible need for new water resources (see section 11). The Government would wish to see the work mirroring progress with the preparation of fresh estimates of current reliable yields.

Demand for Public Water Supplies

Past and current demand

5.1 Between 1 April 1994 and 31 March 1995, water put into public supply in England and Wales averaged 16,489 Ml/d (Water Services Association, 1995). This amount went to meet demand from households and industry. It also included an estimated (Ofwat, 1996a) average of 5,155 Ml/d lost in leakage from water company and customer pipes.

5.2 Figures for water put into public supply over the last 20 years are shown in Table 3 and show a 15% increase from 1974/5 to 1994/5, but only a 3% increase within the last ten years. The figures for water supplied through meters approximately correspond to that supplied to industrial premises and indicate a fall in that component of supply from about 33% of the total in 1974/75 to 25% in 1994/5, probably not only as a result of changing industrial activity but also of greater practice of water conservation measures.

5.3 There are of course regional variations within these trends. Table 4 looks at water put into public supply in each of the 10 former water authority areas in the calendar year 1975, including that supplied by the then statutory water companies operating within each area. It compares these figures with the total water put into supply by the successor companies in 1994/95. There has been no change in the North West, but in the Wessex and South West areas supplies have increased by 30% and 25% respectively. The Southern region shows a 10% increase, while Severn Trent and Thames are very similar at 15% and 16% respectively. Table 5 shows the corresponding figures in each of the five years between 1990/91 and 1994/95.

5.4 A study funded by the Department of the Environment and recently published (Herrington, 1996a) gives estimates of per capita consumption of water for all household purposes as follows:

Year	Per capita consumption (litres/head/day)
1961	85
1971	108
1981	123
1991/92 (April-March)	140

5.5 Although estimates, these figures indicate an annual growth of 2.7% in consumption through the 1960s, with a lower rate of some 1.4% through the 1970s and 1980s. A report (Ofwat, 1996a) from the Office of Water Services (Ofwat) shows the average amongst all water companies of the reported best estimates of per capita consumption for 1994/5 to be 149 litres/head/day (l/h/d), with a range from 128 l/h/d to 180 l/h/d, indicating an annual growth of some 2.1% since 1991/92.

5.6 The major components of the water balance[12] can be measured or estimated with varying degrees of precision. This is routinely done. However, the micro-components of demand for household water supplies – meaning the demand from the various ways in which water is used within households – have not been measured or estimated to the same extent.

5.7 A report (NRA, 1995b) prepared for the NRA has indicated that there is within companies a substantial although disparate body of base information which could be drawn upon for more developed studies of the micro-components of household demand. Water use has been categorised somewhat differently and the various data are confined to particular geographical areas. The extent to which information available from the data can be extrapolated to England and Wales as a whole is not clear. Socio-economic differences in household demand are not yet fully understood, although one published study (Edwards and Martin, 1995) sets out to address this issue.

5.8 Demand studies have also tended to characterise average demands in the various categories of use, rather than short term variations or peak demand. However, a major – but not novel – concern arising in 1995 was the effect of peak demand on existing water supply arrangements. As a contribution to the present review, Ofwat has studied companies' data on the demand for water since January 1993 to the end of 1995 and has published the outcome (Ofwat, 1996b) Some of the key points emerging from this work are:

(a) many companies, although not all, reported record peak demands for water (as measured by distribution input) during the summer of 1995, which in most cases were sustained for longer than in previous years, in correspondence with the prolonged hot summer weather;

(b) an increase in trend amongst consumers towards garden watering can result in high peak demands;

---

12 The "water balance" compares the amount of water put into the distribution system with estimates of that leaving the system, whether through use or leakage. Annex F provides more detailed illustration.

Demand for Public Water Supplies

(c) a reported increase in 1994/95 for some companies in their winter base level of demand may, in some cases, be due to increased leakage; and

(d) water companies need to do more to understand better the demand for water, not least by better recording of its components.

Forecasts of future demand

5.9 Lack of information on the micro-components of either average or peak demand for public water supplies contributes to the difficulty of overall demand forecasting. Demand forecasting has to take account of likely changes in the following aspects:

(a) water-use efficiency of domestic and industrial equipment;

(b) lifestyle of household consumers as it affects their use of water;

(c) industrial and service sector activities;

(d) price and charging methods for water; and

(e) leakage from companies' and customers' pipes.

5.10 Assessment of changes in the first four of these aspects is best informed by a detailed knowledge of the existing components of demand. The matter of leakage is considered in section 9 of this paper. From consideration of the available information, a recent study (Herrington, 1996a) concluded that, excluding leakage, but with allowance for the first three aspects, overall demand on public water supplies in the South East of England would increase by about 25% between 1991 and 2021.

5.11 Forecasts of demand for water were submitted to Ofwat by individual companies in their strategic business plans in March 1994. These were aggregated and summarised in a paper (Ofwat, 1994) prepared by Ofwat in November of that year and predicted an increase of 12.4% in water delivered to households between the forecast levels for 1994/5 and 2014/5. Water delivered to non-households was predicted to decrease by 4.6% in the same period. However, water put into supply was predicted to increase by only 0.6% because of a forecast 20.6% reduction in distribution losses.

5.12 Another recent study (NRA, 1994) considered all five aspects in three different scenarios and arrived at "high", "medium" and "low" demand forecasts giving respectively a 25%, 10% and 2% increase in the same period. With public water supply demand at some 16,700 Ml/d in 1991, these percentages represent some

4,200, 1,700 and 330 Ml/d respectively and encompass the range of the other two predictions just mentioned.

5.13 The underlying demand for water in a particular area will be influenced by the size of the population to be served and by the extent there of water-using industry. These considerations were incorporated within the scenarios developed by the NRA which took account of projected population growth, projected household occupancy and underlying economic activity. Clearly, similar considerations should continue to feature in further assessments of the need for local or strategic new resource development.

5.14 Although the overall trend in industrial demand for public water supplies in the last twenty years is downwards (see paragraph 5.2), desirable new industrial development may lead to significant local increases in demand. Local resident populations can go down as well as up – moves from inner cities since 1945 provide illustration – but decreases in one location lead to increases elsewhere, although perhaps dispersed over a larger area. Overall, the projected population trend in England and Wales is upwards, from 51.10 million in 1991 to 52.99 million in 2001, 54.47 million in 2011 and 55.32 million in 2021 – an increase from 1991 to 2021 of some 8.3%.

5.15 An NRA report (NRA, 1995c) identified demand management options which, if implemented throughout England and Wales, could cumulatively deliver reductions considerably in excess of the 8% increase in demand which this projected population increase at first sight would imply. Nevertheless possible higher localised growth in resident population could outstrip the ability of demand management to contain increased demand for water within the capacity of existing water resources.

5.16 The upward trend in population projections is reflected more strongly in projections for household numbers. From 19.2 million in 1991, the number of all types of households in England is projected to rise by 23% to 23.6 million in 2016. This net projected increase of 4.4 million includes a rise of 3.5 million in the number of single person households, to 8.6 million in 2016. Some commentators see this 70% increase as likely to present an added strain on water supplies, on the plausible assumption that domestic water-using appliances may not be used so efficiently in single person households as in multi-occupancy households. There is as yet limited evidence available with which to test this assumption.

5.17 The need to consider the effect of localised population changes on the provision of water supplies is embodied in the Department of the Environment's Planning Policy Guidance note (DoE, 1992a) on Development Plans and Regional Planning Guidance. Regional Planning Guidance documents prepared by the Government Offices for the regions consider this matter in more detail. This guidance stresses the need for local authorities, water companies and the Environment Agency to work together to ensure that water supply sources are protected and that rates of development do not exceed the capacities of the existing or planned water supply systems to meet the projected demand.

5.18 Given the degree of uncertainties outlined in the previous paragraphs, **the Government's view** is that there is a particular need for water companies to undertake further detailed assessments of how water is used by households in their supply areas in order better to forecast overall demand for water. Each water company should make its own assessment of overall household use and of the extent to which this varies within its supply area. Each water company should also assess the micro-components of water use within households in its supply area. However, in view of the relative complexity of micro-component use assessments, it may be appropriate for some companies to extrapolate information obtained by others, provided the validity of this approach can be demonstrated.

5.19 Programmes for these measurements need careful design and conduct. Some companies already have substantial experience in this and their relevant Associations may wish to consider how this can be disseminated so as to minimise replication of effort. For each company, the programmes must provide adequate coverage of different geographical and socio-economic areas within the company's supply boundaries. A common categorisation of micro-components of water use should be adopted. Both average and peak demand use should be measured. As information is gathered, it should be passed to the Environment Agency and Ofwat and should be made available to other organisations which may have a valid interest. For its part, the Environment Agency has set out in Annex F its views on best practice for demand analysis and forecasting.

5.20 The information base which will eventually accrue will facilitate demand forecasting and thence inform decisions on strategic water resource developments. The information will also assist companies in the execution of their duty to promote the efficient use of water by their customers by providing better indications of how water is used within households. Therefore, the Government considers that all water companies should set up, if they have not already done so, suitable measurement programmes with a view to commencing data gathering by the end of 1997. Data should be made publicly available from each programme as soon as a useful amount has been acquired.

Climate change

5.21 Even with better information on present household demand for water, the accuracy of forecasts of future demand will remain heavily dependent on predictions of economic, lifestyle and cultural changes within the community of consumers. Changes in all three of these considerations are likely to be further influenced by climate change – the CCIRG report reviews the potential effects. Under the CCIRG scenario summarised above (see paragraph 4.14ff), temperature rise and its consequent effects on demand for water might add an additional 5% (some 830 Ml/d) on to what it takes as a predicted 12% increase in the demand on public water supply between 1990 and 2021, due largely to increased usage in gardens, with the potential for much larger increases in peak demand.

5.22 This assessment is broadly in line with that made in another recently published report (Herrington, 1996a) for the Department of the Environment. Both reports point out that these assessments are based on particular scenarios of climate change; other scenarios are plausible which might have significantly different effects on the demand for water. Therefore, it is **the Government's view** that further studies are needed of the implications for demand on public water supplies of climate change scenarios.

5.23 As with assessment of effects on water resources (see paragraph 4.17ff), there is, with the recent CCIRG work now to hand, sufficient information available from the Hadley Centre for an immediate start to be made on these studies. The Government would expect water companies to take the lead, and would see value in a co-operative approach through their Associations and United Kingdom Water Industry Research (UKWIR), the water industry's own research body. This will require close collaboration with centres of excellence; indeed, UKWIR held in June 1996 a very useful seminar for that very purpose. Following this, UKWIR has already met representatives of the Environment Agency and of the Global Atmosphere

Demand for Public Water Supplies

Division and the Water Supply and Regulation Division of the Department of the Environment to plan future work.

5.24 Also as with water resource effects, it will be important to construct from the climate change scenarios a range of possible consequences for water demand. The process will be considerably aided by the more detailed measurements of the micro-components of current demand which the Government wishes to see, and will therefore continue to evolve from the start already made. It should progress at the fastest possible rate.

Demand Management: Introduction

6.1   Section 2 of this paper emphasises the importance to both consumers and the environment of ensuring that effective management arrangements for water resources and supply systems are in place *before* claims are made on new water resources in order to meet demand. The management of demand for water is a vital component of those arrangements. The following three sections consider ways in which the efficiency of water use can be increased, the rôle of charging for water supplies in influencing demand, and the need to control leakage of water from pipes. Between them, the various components offer a package of measures which, by controlling waste and consumption, can be used to manage the total quantity of water abstracted from a source of supply[13].

6.2   It is essential to recognize the interactions between the components. Charging by volume, where it is possible, would, for example, encourage customers to fit water-efficient equipment when they have the opportunity, and to avoid waste – as is evidenced by the approach of many commercial and industrial users now. Regulatory influence on the design of equipment and fittings should help to ensure that customers have an appropriate range of water-efficient devices available to them. Provision of information on water conservation will help to demonstrate to customers the options available to them for helping themselves financially – whether in the short or the longer term – while also benefitting the environment. Demonstrably better leakage control by water companies will help persuade their customers that seeking efficient use of water is an important activity, to be undertaken in the spirit of partnership by all and not simply to be left to the other party.

6.3   It is important to determine and apply the optimum package of demand management measures for each particular water supply system, taking into account the balance between availability of developed resources and the projected changes in demand if no further measures were taken. In some cases, where the balance is favourable and sustainable, the package might be small in comparison with cases where the balance gives cause for concern. The optimum will also be determined by the nature of the customer base in the area – for example, the extent of industrial demand, the mix of types of housing – as well as by the features of the supply system infrastructure. However, for all systems, the approach to demand management will contain the common themes of:

◆   efficient use,

◆   effective and equitable charging arrangements, and

◆   economic levels of leakage.

6.4   Particularly in the light of the probable effects of climate change, **the Government's view** is that the interests of sustainable development and efficient management of water resources and supply require a gradual shift in the longer term towards charging by volume for household use and for use by those commercial premises which continue to be charged in proportion to rateable value. That cannot be achieved quickly or universally, however, and it is essential that moves to charging by volume should be sensitive to customer's attitudes, the practical difficulties, and the relative economic benefits as a whole.

6.5   Demand management is vital, but it is not a panacea against the development of new water resources. Inevitably there are limits to the savings in water consumption which it can ultimately provide in any given situation. Moreover, there are limits to the rate at which those savings can accrue – the speed with which the various measures can be introduced and conducted will be limited by the ability or willingness of those (companies and customers) taking them to do so. Paragraph 11.29ff considers this point further.

---

13   This is the definition of "demand management" offered in the NRA publication "Saving Water" (NRA, 1995c) and reflects the environmental concerns which must be inherent in the effective operation of water resources and supply systems.

Increasing Efficiency of Use

7.1 **The Government believes** that it is essential to pursue water conservation by both voluntary and regulatory means. Water conservation offers considerable scope for avoiding waste with little or no disbenefit to consumers (and positive financial benefit to customers if they are paying in relation to volume consumed). Voluntary action should be encouraged as far as is practicable. But regulatory intervention may be particularly necessary to influence consumption which has little or no marginal cost to customers; provided that regulations are cast in the form of design or performance standards their cost should be low – though the details would be subject to compliance cost and benefit assessment.

7.2 There are three broad areas of activity by which efficiency of water use can be increased:
(a) provision and installation of more water-efficient equipment and fittings,
(b) reduction of leakage and other wastage from customers' pipes and existing fittings; and
(c) promotion of efficient use by customers.

7.3 It is essential to regard these activity areas holistically as offering, in various combinations to suit local circumstances, an effective combined approach to demand management which, where appropriate, need to be used in conjunction with price signals to help provide the right framework of incentives. There is possible scope for further regulatory action to assist both (a) and (b). More can be done through voluntary action by consumers under all three heads.

Provision of more water-efficient equipment and fittings

7.4 Two recent publications (NRA, 1995c; Herrington, 1996a) contain projections of how changes in water-using equipment could influence demand on public water supplies over the next two decades. The greatest scope for water savings are likely to be found in improved design of equipment for personal washing, WC flushing and garden watering, but other items need consideration. The Department of the Environment's 1992 consultation paper "Using Water Wisely" (DoE, 1992b) and the Government's response to that consultation (DoE, 1995a) provide further illustration.

7.5 There is a general trend in **washing machine** and **dishwasher** design towards lower water use, probably driven by construction cost savings if less water is handled and perhaps by energy efficiency and cost considerations. There may be scope for some tightening of water use criteria in new Regulations which will replace the existing Water Byelaws (see paragraph 7.10). Ecolabelled machines may prove increasingly popular, especially if the significance and benefits of ecolabelling are made more widely known through marketing techniques.

7.6 Removal of the current prohibition of new installations of dual flush in **water closets** might offer scope for a reduction in this major component of demand, which accounts for some 30% of household water use (Edwards and Martin, 1995). There may be scope for further reductions, both by improved design of the siphonic valve devices conventionally used in this country and by introduction of the flushing valve devices (which deliver water at mains pressure) or drop valves encountered elsewhere in Europe. Accelerated demand reductions by means of the introduction of more water-efficient water closets might be achieved by financial incentives for customers to change or modify existing installations. The 'quick fix' solution of reducing existing cistern capacity by inserting a suitable object are generally effective provided capacity is not reduced to such an extent that double flushing become necessary to clear the pan. Incentives for modifications to urinal flush systems are already considerable since most are in metered properties, but there may be scope for tightening prescriptions in the new Water Regulations.

7.7 Demand from **personal washing** is likely to increase because of expected increased shower ownership, higher showering frequencies and greater use of 'power showers' (Herrington,1996a). Water conservation could come through ecolabelling of equiment.

7.8 Household external uses are dominated by garden watering. Some manufacturers are already adopting voluntarily potentially water-saving features (for example, spring-action hosepipes or timed sprinklers) and their use should be encouraged. Micro irrigation systems and soaker hoses should give more efficient use of water provided they are correctly employed. Other means of minimising increases in external use demand include public education campaigns featuring advice from independent expert bodies (see paragraph 7.21), and volumetric charging for garden watering.

7.9 **Used water recycling** may be capable of development in large, quasi-domestic properties such as hotels and hostels where the scale of the operation may make it cost-effective. Some devices for recycling in individual households are beginning to appear, but their present cost is such that they may not be attractive to householders in comparison with any savings in water charges which are likely to accrue. In all cases, systems would need to deliver a recycled water acceptable to residents in its aesthetic properties. There is considerable scope here for further innovation on the part of manufacturers, in order both to bring down the cost of installations and also to achieve acceptability in wider terms for this relatively novel approach to water efficiency.

Proposed regulatory action in respect of fittings and equipment

7.10 The current Water Byelaws, which include regulations on water use for water conservation purposes, are due to be replaced with new Regulations made under section 74 of the Water Industry Act 1991 (see paragraph 22 of Annex B). The intention is that these should contain less detailed prescription, with general requirements supported by approved documents setting out ways in which those requirements might be met. A consultation paper (DoE, 1995b) provides details of options under consideration.

7.11 The Chairman and membership of the Government's Water Regulations Advisory Committee was announced on 17 July 1996. Its terms of reference are to advise the Secretary of State for the Environment on the requirements for plumbing installations and fittings to be included in the new Regulations and on other technical matters connected with them. The Committee started its work in September 1996 and will establish its own detailed work timetable, but the expectation is that new Regulations will be in force by late 1998.

7.12 The use of regulations on water conservation is most justified where, in their absence, decisions having long term implications for water use are unlikely to reflect consideration of the economics of supply. This might apply, for example, to the design of water closets, shower design requirements, and hosepipes for domestic purposes. Consideration is being given to the incorporation of water conservation requirements within the new Regulations. The Committee is being asked to look widely at this question. Equipment manufacturers will need to build on their expertise in identifying and responding to the opportunities which this exercise will provide for assisting water conservation.

Wastage from customers' pipes and existing fittings

7.13 In the light of their experiences from the summer of 1995 onwards, several companies are currently offering to repair leaks in customers' pipes either free of charge or at greatly discounted cost. This is a sensible step, particularly in areas where supplies are at risk. It will be for companies to decide on the precise nature, extent and duration of such schemes.

7.14 Examples from overseas have been reported (NRA, 1995c; Herbertson and Howarth, 1996) of the distribution to consumers of "self-help" packs to improve efficiency of water use by existing domestic fittings. These might contain easily-installed flow restrictors, re-washering kits, low-volume shower heads or cistern volume reducers, but the precise contents of the packs would need to be determined according to local circumstances such that there could be no risk to water quality or of actually increasing water use (as might result from inappropriate reduction in cistern volume). Self-help packs might also contain easily-comprehensible advice on other steps which customers could reasonably take to improve efficiency of use.

7.15 Companies should take these steps. However, both are dependent for their success in preventing wastage on the willingness of consumers to respond. The manner in which the availability of leak repair services or self-help packs is communicated by companies will significantly determine this willingness, but the various consumers' organisations and other groups with an interest may have an important rôle to play in encouraging consumers to respond constructively.

Efficient use by customers

7.16 Since 1 February 1996, water companies have had a statutory duty to promote the efficient use of water by their customers (see paragraph 20 of Annex B). The Director General of Water Services conducted an initial survey of how companies intend to carry out this new duty and asked them to submit formal strategies to him by 1 October 1996. These will be considered in the light of each company's circumstances and the views of other interested organisations. They will be published and companies will be required to submit annual reports on progress against them to the Director. He has the power to require water undertakers to take specific action or to achieve specific overall standards of performance in respect of the promotion of efficient use of water, and to take enforcement action if those requirements are not met. Annex G, contributed by Ofwat, sets out some general principles

Increasing Efficiency of Use

which, in the Director's view, should feature in companies' plans in respect of this duty.

7.17 One means of giving effect to the duty is for water companies to collaborate in establishing programmes of education in water saving on a regional basis wider than their own individual supply areas, or indeed for England and Wales as a whole. The extent and financing of such collaborative programmes would be matters for companies' decision, taking into account the benefits which would accrue for customers and shareholders.

7.18 A further means of promoting efficient use of water is for water companies to take steps to encourage customers to install more water-efficient equipment. Left to normal replacement rates for water-using equipment, which are for the most part dictated by the equipment's design life or the design life of its surroundings, accrual of consumption savings through increasing use of more water-efficient designs will be slow. Dependent on the success of consumer information and education campaigns, a faster rate may be obtained. Further acceleration may be possible through the introduction or demonstration of direct financial benefits.

7.19 There have been some calls for the establishment of a 'Water Savings Trust', funded either through general levy by water companies on all their customers or by the Government from taxpayers, to provide domestic customers with grants for such installations. It will be recognised that, in the absence of widespread volumetric charging, only a small minority of domestic customers would have the prospect of reduced water charges as an incentive to seek grants and that they would thereby benefit in a way which would be unavailable to the majority. However, water companies might consider whether it would benefit the whole body of customers to promote grant-aided installation of water-efficient equipment and fittings to all customers in particular areas as a significant contribution, through demand management, to the deferral or removal of the need for new water resource development and the attendant implications for water charges.

7.20 There may be other, less direct means of influencing household demand. Some sections of the community might be especially sympathetic to direct appeals for water conservation on environmental grounds where rising demand might otherwise result in environmentally-controversial development of new resources.

Others might be influenced incidentally to conserve water if they were to perceive benefits to their energy bills from using less hot water.

7.21 Organisations independent of the water industry have an important rôle to play in educating consumers about aspects of efficient use of water. The Royal Horticultural Society (RHS) already provides guidance on effective and efficient garden watering to its members and enquirers, and has worked jointly with the Water Services Association to produce a free leaflet entitled "the water friendly garden" of which over half a million copies have been distributed. Many water companies have also produced their own advice on garden watering, in some cases using the broadcast media to convey the information.

7.22 The CBI has produced a booklet entitled "Efficient water management – Guidelines for business" aimed at increasing business awareness of water conservation. Scope for savings was demonstrated in the Aire and Calder project, initiated in March 1992 by the Centre for Exploitation of Science and Technology, a charitable body funded by industry and government. This featured 11 companies, all discharging to the River Aire or the River Calder in Yorkshire, and was aimed at the reduction of emissions through waste minimisation and the adoption of cleaner technology. However, by February 1994 the participants had between them already achieved annual savings of some £190,000 through reduced demand for water supplies and had identified the potential for further annual savings of about £460,000.

7.23 The Government's Environmental Technology Best Practice Programme (jointly funded by the Department of the Environment and the Department of Trade and Industry) promotes the use of better environmental practices, helps reduce waste and hence business costs for UK industry and commerce. Since its launch in 1994, several publications have been produced which are relevant to efficient water use in industry and commerce, including, earlier this year, a general guide (Environmental Technology Best Practice Programme, 1996) on reducing water use. Other publications relevant to efficient water use are in preparation or planned under the Programme, which is also monitoring the progress of several new regional waste minimisation clubs[14].

---

14   Information on publications and events under the Environmental Technology Best Practice Programme can be obtained on its Environmental Helpline, 0800 585794.

7.24 Much is already being done, particularly by industry and commerce, to increase efficiency of water use and avoid waste; and much is being done to inform consumers of the action that they can take. **The Government's view** is that renewed effort in these activities would be beneficial, drawing on a range of short- and longer-term options to suit local circumstances and recognising the added incentive for water conservation which volumetric charging provides. For its part, the Government will work with the water companies and their regulators, manufacturers of water-using equipment and fittings, and organisations representing water consumers to explore additional ways in which its Best Practice programmes and other techniques used successfully to implement its environmental management and energy efficiency policies can be used to encourage more efficient use of water.

Charging for Water Supplies

8.1 The evidence both from England and Wales and from abroad is that voluntary and regulatory action to encourage water conservation and efficiency of use needs to be combined where possible by financial incentives. Here, however, use of those incentives must take into account public attitudes and the distributional impact of movement from a system of household charging which entails a high degree of cross-subsidy between customers.

8.2 It is for water companies to decide the basis on which they will charge their customers, subject to the Director General of Water Services' supervision to ensure that pricing is not unduly discriminatory or preferential (see paragraph 24 of Annex B). **The Government believes** however that the gradual extension of metering in combination with the development of more sophisticated tariff structures policy has an essential rôle to play in managing demand for water and ensuring sustainable water usage against the background of climate change and the growing use of water by households for purposes other than drinking and essential hygiene.

8.3 In general, the introduction of metering should be selective, and voluntary in respect of the occupiers who are now charged in their present properties on the basis of rateable values. It also needs to be applied sensitively in respect of those who have high use for essential household purposes. But new properties should continue to be fitted with meters as the norm, as should those which have high external use for garden-watering and swimming pools. Where an occupier moves to a dwelling with a meter, charging should be on a metered basis. The metering of all commercial and industrial properties should gradually be completed.

8.4 Currently, some 92% of household customers pay for their water supplies on the basis of the rateable value of the property they occupy. As is well known, this system bears very little relation to the volume of water consumed by the occupants. The same would be true of any other charging system based on property values. The Government has made clear its view that a shift in England and Wales to charging on the basis of Council Tax banding of properties would have very significant implications for the bills of many who occupy dwellings in the lower Council Tax bands. For this and other reasons it does not intend to enable local authorities to release to water companies information on the Council Tax banding of properties for the purpose of

developing a water charging system. In order to facilitate a gradual extension of metering on the basis outlined in paragraph 8.3 without disruptive changes from one basis of charging to a second and then to a third, it has said that it will seek legislation to enable rateable values to continue to be used after 31 March 2000.

Charging by volume consumed

8.5 Charging by measured volume of water used is the only means of directly relating charge to consumption and thence to cost of supply. Only this approach can realistically provide appropriate financial incentive for customers to use water more efficiently. However, the extent to which it does so will depend in a complex fashion on the way in which the measurements are related to charges through tariff structures and on the affluence, preferences and lifestyle of the customers.

8.6 There is extensive domestic and international evidence of the impact of charging by volume on water usage.

8.7 Trials of charging domestic customers by metering were conducted between 1988 and 1992 in 12 areas of England (National Metering Trials Working Group, 1993). The estimated overall reduction in water consumption in each area is shown in Table 6, together with the form of tariff to which customers were subject. The average reduction in the 11 small trial areas was 10.8%, but with a range from an apparent increase of 1.6% to a reduction of 17.2%.

8.8 The twelfth and only large trial area encompassed the whole of the Isle of Wight. This trial was conducted primarily to understand the logistics of large scale metering. Data on water put into supply indicated a reduction in water put into supply of 21.3%. However, just under half this figure came from reductions in supply pipe leakage and similar savings have since been achieved in unmetered parts of the water company's area by enhanced leakage control.

8.9 A collation of twenty-two studies worldwide of the effect of charging by metering on domestic consumption showed reductions in consumption generally between 10% and 30% (OECD, 1987). A recent paper (Herrington, 1996b) further collates the 1987 material with more detailed results of the 1988-1992 trials and also with results from earlier trials in the UK to produce a tabulated summary of the effect of charging domestic customers by metering on peak demand. This indicates that peak consumption may be reduced by between 25% and 35% in relatively hot summers.

8.10 Data on comparative consumption in metered and non-metered areas in the summer of 1995 have not yet been assessed. However, there are some indications that areas significantly penetrated by meters have experienced peak demands lower than those in broadly comparable areas with lower metering penetration. The recent Ofwat report on water demand (Ofwat, 1996b) provides some illustration of this.

8.11 One question frequently debated in the United Kingdom is whether the reduction in usage, and in leakage on the customer's side, that accompanies the introduction of metering is short-lived. Significant caution in water use might be expected immediately on the introduction of a meter, because the customer is uncertain about the impact on the bill in comparison with the earlier bills. The customer may be less cautious with experience, but the weight of evidence is that the introduction of charging by volume induces a step reduction in consumption, so that the underlying increase in overall consumption related to lifestyle changes (if there is one) proceeds on a new parallel but lower track – that is to say, the re-attainment of the level of overall consumption attained immediately before the introduction of meters occurs only after a period.

8.12 The possible impact of water metering on large, low-income households and on households where there is high water use for medical reasons is frequently raised as an objection to charging by metered volume. However, an investigation (WS Atkins, 1992) carried out into the social impact of domestic metering in the 12 trial areas in England (see paragraph 8.7) suggests that this is not an extensive problem; 8% of the sample of households perceived difficulty in affording their water bills after metering but social or financial hardship was identified by the survey in less than half (3.8%) of these. Some such households may feel that they must be extremely cautious in water use when they first encounter charging by meter and adopt undesirable approaches to toilet flushing and bathing, although there is no evidence that health problems have resulted. It should be noted that other household essentials like heating and lighting are charged for by meter. It is in principle preferable to deal with the needs of high-use, low-income households through income-related arrangements rather than to determine the whole basis of charging water solely with respect to those needs.

Metering strategies

8.13 Subject only to the Director General of Water Services' powers against undue preferential or discrimi-

natory pricing, water companies are free to tailor their metering strategies using whatever incentives they consider most appropriate in their circumstances. The Government looks to water companies to develop tariff structures which encourage the efficient use of water, and to the regulators to use their powers to encourage that. The views of Ofwat on what constitutes best practice in this respect are summarised in Annex H.

8.14 One obvious strategy is to increase metering of those household customers who, through high discretionary use, contribute most to the average demand, the peak demand, or both. Some companies, as a result of their experiences in 1995, have already focused their metering efforts on garden sprinkler users. The effect will depend on local circumstances, but generally can be expected to offer lower demand (both peak and average) together with an income stream for the company from customers who nevertheless continue with high water use.

8.15 Care is needed in detailed application of the approach, but **the Government's view** is that selective extension of metering to aid demand management amongst customers with an actual or potential high use of water is an appropriate step for water companies to take, and should be pursued urgently by those companies which have not already done so.

8.16 The extent of penetration of metering may be governed by concerns over the cost of meter installation and of the subsequent meter reading operation. Leaving aside consideration of the level of metering technology to be installed and the short and long term distribution of metering costs amongst customers, the issue can be seen, from one perspective, as fundamentally one of the costs of metering in comparison with the costs to the customer and the environment which will accrue if the demand savings which are likely to result from metering are not obtained.

8.17 So far as average demand is concerned, the question ultimately is whether development of a new resource can be significantly deferred – or even avoided – by demand savings amongst customers encouraged in that regard by the introduction of metering. The question is the same in respect of peak demand, but with the added consideration that, regardless of resource availability, need for enlargement of treatment and/or distribution system capacity might be avoided or mitigated by a move to charging by meter.

Charging for Water Supplies

8.18 These questions have to be addressed by water companies in the light of the circumstances in their own areas. In doing so, it is clearly necessary that the full costs of meter installation on the one hand, and of infrastructure improvements on the other, are estimated, taking into account the scope for economies of scale in the former and the environmental costs associated with the latter. In so doing, companies may very well arrive at optimum levels of domestic metering penetration which will differ between and within their areas.

Tariff structures

8.19 The demand management potential of charging by volume could be significantly reinforced by tariff structures which take into account seasonal and daily variations in pressure of demand. More sophisticated structures would allow charges to be more closely related to costs of particular sorts of supply – for example, to those of meeting peak demand – and avoid imposing charges on those not giving rise to the costs, in contrast to the effect of averaging under present arrangements. There is however as yet little evidence of significant innovation or experimentation in this respect – even within the confines of existing water meter capability – within the water industry, beyond the 1988-92 trials in England.

8.20 Tariff structures could be based on fixed rates of standing charge and measured use, irrespective of times, seasons or extent of use. Or they could be relatively complex, incorporating increasing charging rates for step increments in use together with rates varying according to season, week or even time of day. Annex H provides a further discussion by Ofwat of various options and Annex C reviews some experiences in other countries.

8.21 If there were no constraints arising from meter measurement capability, ease of meter reading or computation of charge, tariff design would be dictated by the intended objectives of the introduction of charging by meter. For example, if in order to reflect costs the objectives were mainly concerned with minimising peak demand, a relatively complex tariff based upon season or even meteorological conditions could be envisaged. If peak demand were to be of lesser concern than average demand, a more simple tariff might suffice.

8.22 There are particular concerns over the potential impact of metering on low-income households. Tariff structures offer the opportunity of giving some protection to water use for essential hygiene purposes by means of an initial block of water at a flat rate – though this cannot be carried so far as to undermine the general principle of payment in relation to consumption.

8.23 **The Government's view** is that consideration should be given to the development of more sophisticated tariff structures as a means of optimising demand management through water charges. Individual water companies need to take the initiative, drawing upon relevant experiences of water supply organisations elsewhere and with a clear objective for each tariff structure to meet. The result should be consumption-related structures which reflect particular characteristics of customers (but without being unduly preferential or discriminatory – see paragraph 24 of Annex B) while at the same time contributing to demand management. The Government hopes for rapid progress, consistent with the need for consultation with customers and Ofwat, especially in areas where existing water resources are under strain.

8.24 Meter reading capability is a constraint in moving beyond the most simple forms of tariff. Most meters already installed do not lend themselves to automated or remote reading methods and are incapable of the frequency of measurement which would be needed to sustain a diurnally-varying tariff. While current manual reading methods could notionally sustain at least a crude seasonal tariff structure, the manpower costs involved might be prohibitive.

8.25 It may be that in response to an emerging market meter measuring and meter reading technology could rapidly develop to meet cost-effectively the needs inherent in more sophisticated tariff structures. What is certain is that the technology is unlikely to develop in this way unless there is seen to be a clear need for it. Such clarity could only emerge from detailed studies and dialogue between manufacturers and the prospective customer water companies.

8.26 Other benefits might result from improved meter technology. A reliable remote reading capability would remove the difficulty of physical access to meters and the related concerns about the convenience and security of customers. "Smart" meters could allow information about property type and occupancy to be transmitted and updated if these were relevant to the charging structure. There is also the prospect of combined utility meter reading – something of particular relevance to the emerging " multi-utilities".

8.27 The Government's view is that, in the interests of ensuring sustainable water usage, water meter technology needs to develop further in order to facilitate cost-effectively the introduction of more sophisticated tariff structures. Water companies, either individually or co-operatively, need to pursue this with existing or potential manufacturers, in the light of their consideration of the part which such sophistication might play in contributing to demand management.

Tariffs for industrial use

8.28 About 73% of industrial users of public water supplies are already metered, but those users account for some 90% of industrial consumption However, industrial tariffs have potential for innovation in much the same way as discussed above. A further possibility for industrial tariffs is that they might be set at a lower rate for particular customers in return for the acceptance that, at times of actual or predicted high demand, the industrial supply might be reduced or interrupted. This is a matter for negotiation between industrial customers and water companies. The former can no doubt be expected to take into account the implications of interruptions of supply for their businesses and employees, and to make appropriate alternative arrangements if necessary.

Leakage

9.1 Water which leaks from mains, supply pipes and customers' equipment unnecessarily and uneconomically represents straightforward waste, and a resource which could be used to meet consumers' needs without making additional calls on water resources. In the interests of consumers and the protection of the environment, leakage should be reduced to the economic level in the particular circumstances. In principle, that level is the lowest that can be achieved without incurring more combined capital and operating costs than would be necessary to provide an equivalent supply from a new water resource, including the cost of protecting the environment to an appropriate extent against the effects of the necessary new withdrawal. The economic level of leakage, by definition, varies with the particular circumstances of each supply system and has to be calculated in each case. Within this framework, leakage control should be used in conjunction with the other demand management measures in an optimum mix for each system of supply.

Expression and significance of leakage

9.2 Considerable attention was focused on leakage from the water distribution system as the 1995 drought developed and water use restrictions loomed. Ofwat published in May 1996 a report (Ofwat, 1996a) on leakage of water in England and Wales. This showed that total leakage was about 30% of the water put into distribution systems, with leakage from companies' pipes accounting for 23% of the distribution input and 7% leaking from customers' supply pipes.

9.3 Companies are concerned that expression of leakage as a percentage of distribution input does not properly reflect their circumstances and makes for invidious comparison between companies. The National Leakage Initiative (NLI) set up in 1991 jointly by the Water Services Association and the Water Companies Association recommended (UK Water Industry, 1994) distribution losses to be expressed in terms of volume per length of distribution system per day, with the length of distribution system including not only the length of mains but also an allowance for estimated length of communication pipes. The NLI also recognised that expression of distribution losses in terms of litres per property per day may be a more useful measure, particularly in urban areas. Ofwat reports accordingly feature all three modes of expression of leakage. More recently, the interim report of the House of Commons Environment Committee (Environment Committee, 1996) has drawn attention to the need for unambiguous reporting of leakage levels.

9.4 Whilst there is some technical merit in using these alternative measures to illustrate the extent of leakage from a particular company's distribution system, public attention is reasonably more focused on the simple question of how much of the water put into the system is lost before it reaches customers' premises. Although this may not provide an accurate indicator of stewardship of the company, it is significant in determining whether the demand for water to be put into supply can be met by available resources.

9.5 For example, a leakage component of 30 Ml/d in a total demand of 100 Ml/d upon a resource with a reliable yield of 120 Ml/d would not be critical to the security of supply, but a leakage component of 15 Ml/d in a total demand of 100 Ml/d clearly could be critical if the reliable yield of the resource were to be reduced also to 100 Ml/d. In other words, a leakage of 30% of the distribution input, although undesirable in presentational terms and possibly giving rise to a financial loss, would not have the significance for security of supply in the first case that a leakage of 15% would have in the second.

Economic levels of leakage

9.6 This simple consideration leads on to the much more complex matter of determining the economic level of leakage. This concept reflects the fact that, below a certain level of leakage, the costs of detecting and repairing leakage will be greater than the benefits arising from the water saved.

9.7 The concept of an economic level of leakage is becoming more frequently used by commentators from all perspectives. The 10 water companies then comprising the Water Services Association announced in October 1995 a commitment to `seeking to achieve the lowest levels of leakage that best practice suggests are both technically feasible and economically sensible'.

9.8 Although simple in concept, economic levels of leakage are in practice difficult to determine with accuracy. Costs of leakage control and of water saved can only be estimated from their various component costs, which may themselves be estimates. Moreover, except perhaps for a few small companies, neither the benefit from the water saved nor the cost of leakage control will be the same in all areas. Factors affecting leakage control costs will include the size, age and material of the distribution system, together with topographical details and manpower costs. The cost of water saved will depend, *inter alia*, on the nature of the water resource and should also incorporate allowance for the development of additional resource if that existing is at its limit. Whether or not additional resource is needed, the cost of water should also incorporate the cost to the environment of the existing abstraction and subsequent pumping and treatment.

9.9 The NLI report (UK Water Industry, 1994) considers in some detail the issues involved in determining economic levels of leakage. It proposes a methodology for doing so, but there are gaps and inconsistencies in the extent to which this is followed by individual water companies. Indeed, the Director General of Water Services commented in his recent report (Ofwat, 1996a) that he had 'yet to see a practical and quantified example of the application of the methodology'.

9.10 The water industry had already recognised the difficulties. In October 1995 it commissioned through UKWIR further research, aimed at refining the approach to determining economic levels of leakage. Preliminary recommendations from this research became available to the industry in August 1996.

9.11 The actual proportion of water lost will vary from day to day according to flow and pressure in the system, and will also vary in different parts of the system according to its age, material, number of connections and junctions, and also according to the nature of the terrain which it serves. Determination of the economic level of leakage will help companies to focus their leakage control efforts on the parts of the system which will yield the greatest benefit from leakage reduction.

Managing leakage

9.12 Although the volume of water put into supply is known by companies with a high degree of accuracy, estimates of total leakage are inherently less accurate, all the more so since they require separate estimation of leakage from the company-owned distribution system and of leakage from customers' supply pipes.

9.13 The National Leakage Initiative provided a wide-ranging compendium of information, methodology and advice for water companies on managing leakage. It is appropriate to record that this work itself built upon the solid foundation of a report (NWC, 1980) published some 16 years ago and that therefore much of the more recent material is not novel. However, it appears that, despite these origins, companies are not uniformly content with the NLI approach and that there remains a disparity of practice

and achievement in leakage estimation and control, although further enhancement of methodology is being sought from current work conducted by UKWIR.

9.14 Given this disparity and the various uncertainties attaching to estimates of leakage, companies' intentions and targets for leakage control may be misunderstood or misrepresented, not only between companies and their regulators, customers and opinion-formers, but also within companies. In view of the attention focused upon this issue, and the new commitments given by various companies individually and severally, it is all the more important that leakage levels and targets for their reduction be established and communicated as unambiguously as possible. Without clear communication and evidence of achievement of leakage targets, consumers are likely to remain unimpressed by calls for water conservation on their part.

9.15 **The Government's view** is that, building on existing work, water companies need to:

(a) apply on a consistent basis methods for estimating and expressing leakage levels;

(b) assess economic levels of leakage, taking full account of environmental costs; and

(c) adopt clear programmes and targets for leakage control to economic levels, with rigorous procedures for assessment and reporting of progress in meeting them.

9.16 Action to refine methods for estimating and expressing leakage needs to be continued by the water companies, working jointly through expert working groups or by commissioning further research. The Director General of Water Services has stated (Ofwat, 1996a) that Ofwat will continue to monitor the robustness of companies' water balance estimates and that reporting requirements on companies in their annual returns to Ofwat have been further refined accordingly. Data on leakage within individual supply zones should also be made available by water companies to the Environment Agency for resource planning purposes and to support applications for water abstraction licences.

9.17 Similarly, action to assess the economics of leakage control needs to be taken by each company, drawing on methodology already available (UK Water Industry, 1994) and recently further refined (see paragraph 9.10) as a result of additional research. The Director General of Water Services has stated (Ofwat,

Leakage

1996a) that he expects companies to adopt best practice for leakage economics and to update leakage targets and strategies as appropriate, as part of their demonstration that they are managing their distribution systems in an efficient and prudent manner. Annex I sets out some views from Ofwat on current best practice on leakage control.

9.18 Ofwat has published (Ofwat, 1996a) the leakage targets which each water company expects to achieve by 1997/98, expressed in Ml/d, l/property/d and m^3/km/d, but comments that there is still a degree of uncertainty around some companies' targets and states that the Director is in discussion with those companies. If he were to find the targets not defensible by reference to the achievements of comparable companies,

he has indicated that he would take this into account in setting price limits. He would also consider enforcement action under section 37 of the Water Industry Act 1991, using the provisions of sections 38 and 39 (see paragraph 6 of Annex B).

9.19 Many water companies have themselves published their longer term plans for leakage reduction and some have reported significant improvement in the short term. With so much attention focused on this single issue, it is clearly in water companies' best interests to make clear both their intentions and their achievements in leakage control, as a vital part of both their overall demand management plans and also of their public relations strategy.

Availability of Water Resources and Security of Supply

10.1 Against the background of the foregoing analysis, it is possible to consider questions relating to the balance between available water resources and demand, on the assumption that demand and water supply systems will be well managed on the lines discussed in the preceding sections.

The balance between supply and demand

10.2 The present situation of water resources for public supply in England and Wales is shown in Table 7. This information, produced by the NRA, indicates each of the eight NRA regions to be in a position of surplus based on the average demands experienced over the last five years, although it must be recognised that these surpluses do not exist evenly in each region. The effect of the increased demand arising from the hot summer of 1995 can be seen. The surpluses in some cases suggest that some supply systems could come under significant pressure as demand increases.

10.3 Table 7 updates the 1991 information contained in the NRA publication "Water: Nature's Precious Resource" (NRA, 1994). This publication summarised the reliable yields of water resources in each region and went on to list possible local resource developments. A total reliable yield equivalent to some 20,700 Ml/d was available in England and Wales in 1991 and a further yield of some 2,050 Ml/d was likely to be available for development from local, non-strategic schemes. This analysis did not take into account the possible effects of climate change.

10.4 The NRA publication went on to consider the likely water resources position up to the year 2021. It did this by constructing three scenarios. These are summarised in Table 8 and make assumptions about growth of per capita consumption as well as savings resulting from improved leakage control and increasing penetration of water charging by meter. The assessments of possible imbalances between resources and demand under each scenario were made on the basis of centres of demand for water rather than simply on a company or regional basis. The overall demands for England and Wales which would arise under these three scenarios are shown in Table 9. Table 10 shows the resource deficits which would exist in 2021 under each of the scenarios. Under the "High" demand scenario an overall deficit equivalent to 1,093 Ml/d would result; under the "Low" scenario this would be reduced to 5 Ml/d.

Security of supply

10.5 The balance point between the availability of water resources and the demand for water to be supplied is defined by the desired security of the water supply system against failure. If the desire is that the system should not fail in any way under the worst drought conditions ever recorded, a smaller demand can be balanced against the available resource than would be the case if partial or complete failure were to be considered tolerable in the more extreme recorded circumstances. If the supply were desired to be proof against failure in drought conditions even more severe than previously encountered, the demand which could be balanced would be even smaller.

10.6 No uniform standards in respect of security of water supplies currently exist. For England and Wales, "Levels of Service" in this respect are assessed by Ofwat against companies' own criteria, which typically include the following:

(a) hosepipe bans being needed no more frequently than one year in 10, on average;

(b) drought orders restricting water use should be implemented no more frequently than one year in 50, on average; and

(c) standpipes or rota cuts should be implemented no more frequently than one year in 100, on average.

10.7 These criteria have their origins in general past practice by professionals in the water industry in designing the security of water supply systems on behalf of consumers rather than necessarily in consultation with them. The criteria apply 'on average' and thus do not exclude the possibility of two or more adverse events occurring in a relatively short period. Another drawback, which has been the subject of much comment in concern in the 1995 drought, is that they imply that standpipes or rota cuts are tolerable, albeit at low frequency.

10.8 One of the clearest lessons from the 1995 drought is that the public generally no longer considers the prospect of standpipes or rota cuts to be tolerable, if indeed it ever did. While there are indications that the public may be somewhat more tolerant towards the periodic imposition of hosepipe bans as a means of dealing with shortage of supplies, there can be no assurance either of the extent of this sentiment or of its continuance. Customers in areas with hosepipe bans applied in the majority of recent years might reasonably question whether the water supply system is efficient and secure.

Availability of Water Resources and Security of Supply

10.9 Taken to its logical conclusion, the apparent present-day sentiment in respect of supply interruptions would imply that water supply systems should be designed to be absolutely proof against any conceivable shortage of the raw material. Whether or not such a level of security of supply is technically capable of realisation, it is unlikely that many customers would regard the resulting implications for prices as acceptable.

10.10 In addressing the issue of design standards for security of supply in the light of recent events, and in tacit recognition of the unattainable ideal, there are calls for the establishment of mandatory standards, set at a level and in terms which will provide consumers with added reassurance. But such calls still beg the question of what would constitute "added reassurance", "acceptable security of supply", "tolerable incidence of restrictions", or any other related concept, and do not consider the cost implications of attaining these undefined goals. These calls also leave open the question of whether there should be a single standard for uniform application or whether local variation would be appropriate.

10.11 In principle, security of supply is an aspect of the overall quality of service to the consumer; as with all matters of quality, there is an accompanying price tag. In a competitive, well-informed market, the customer makes a judgment about quality (ideally including environmental considerations) on the one hand and price on the other, and chooses what he or she considers to be an appropriate balance between them. In the case of regulated industries, it is for the price regulator to stand on behalf of customers and reach what he or she considers to be an appropriate balance, in line with his or her judgment of the wishes of the customer whose interest the regulator exists to protect. It is for the regulator to decide whether that balance should be struck at the national level, or could reasonably vary from company to company or system to system.

10.12 There is therefore a strong case for dialogue and debate on these matters between companies, their consumers, and the regulator. It is important that this process should be adequately informed, for it needs to take into account not only the costs of attaining or maintaining a given level of security, but also the more subjective question of consumers' views of the value to them of security of supply. The process of course will necessarily assume that the required quality standards (see paragraph 10.23f) will be met at all times and will be founded upon recognition of the vital importance of water supplies for public health (see paragraph 2.8). Whilst it would appear that nearly all consumers would value highly security against the imposition of standpipes or rota cuts, opinions may be more divided on the value of security against restrictions on non-essential use or hosepipe bans.

10.13 As already noted, the "standards" previously used have been a matter of professional custom and practice and were not statutorily or administratively endorsed. The reliable yields of water resource systems, discussed in section 4, have been estimated against that background, and in practice many systems have been found to be more robust. But just as there is now an emerging need for yields to be freshly estimated (see paragraph 4.9ff), so the opportunity could be taken, with the benefit of modern hydrological techniques, to estimate what security of supply each discrete water resource system is capable of delivering from its reliable yield. In other words, the question would be:

… what, given each particular current system – its past hydrological data, the likely impact of climate change, and projected demands upon it – is the level of security of supply which it affords?

10.14 Such estimates could then be used to inform dialogue with consumers. Some systems might be agreed to have such a high level of security that there is no need of improvement within the projected period under consideration. For other systems which are agreed to be in need of improved security, estimates of the cost of improvement would be needed to inform the ensuing debate. It could be that agreed necessary improvements in some systems could be achieved by relatively modest capital schemes for existing resources or distribution systems. Other cases might feature new resource development and in these the best estimates of the full environmental cost of improvement would be needed.

10.15 This "bottom up" process would have the merit of further inspiring the fresh estimation of the capabilities of existing resources. With appropriate conduct, it could give both companies and their customers a sense of ownership of the question and its eventual solution which would be largely lacking in the "top down" approach of uniform standards, whether mandatory or not.

10.16 Accordingly, **the Government's view** is that there is a need for greater dialogue between water companies and their customers on the balance to be struck between higher security of supply and higher costs.

Availability of Water Resources and Security of Supply

This dialogue should start from a fresh estimate and clear communication of the existing capabilities of each discrete water resource and supply system, against the background of maximum economic use of demand management.

10.17 This dialogue should be conducted by each individual company with its customers. The Customer Service Committees of Ofwat have a clear rôle to play in this process, as have other organisations which are able to represent the views of consumer groups within particular areas. Annex J sets out the views of Ofwat on wider matters which have a bearing on this issue.

Funding security of supply

10.18 Future funding for resolving any security of water supply issues would naturally be an issue for the next Periodic Review of water prices by the Director General of Water Services. The Director will need to consider the financing of investment in improving security of supply alongside other priorities for water company investment and the overall impact on prices to consumers. This consideration leads the Government to hope that the process of dialogue would enable each company to assimilate its customers' wishes and to convey them within a timescale which would depend on the Director's intentions for the timing of his next review.

10.19 There is no fundamental obstacle to companies drawing up and initiating schemes to improve security of supplies at any time to deal with any immediately-pressing problems that may emerge. This is demonstrated by the schemes which several companies have rapidly put in place in the light of their experiences in 1995 and which have had no short-term effect on prices although they amount in total to over £400 million of capital expenditure. Indeed, to the extent that failure to improve security of supplies might result in a breach of the enforceable duty to maintain supplies, companies have little choice in the matter. The treatment of such expenditure in the longer run in relation to price limits is a matter for the Director General of Water Services to consider when he reviews the company's price level in the normal way.

Drought orders and permits

10.20 As companies' actions taken in response to the 1995 drought have shown and are continuing to show, there is a wide range of measures which can be taken, in various combinations, to improve security of supply. The range embraces leakage reduction, introduction of metering for some high users, and promotion of efficient use. It also extends to fast-track major engineering schemes.

10.21 However, it will also be widely recognised that security of supply has been aided by companies obtaining drought orders which have not involved restrictions on water use by consumers, but which authorise only increased abstraction or reduction in compensation water flows from reservoirs. Such drought orders (and, since April 1996, drought permits (see paragraph 35 of Annex B), provide a necessary mechanism for managing water resources limited by exceptional shortage of rainfall. However, recourse to these measures should not be seen by water companies as a means of improving security of supply which it is reasonable to contemplate without having first taken all other measures to provide adequate security of supply in both the short and longer term.

10.22 Drought Orders, whether or not involving restrictions on water use by consumers, are granted only after careful consideration of all the issues which statutory consultees and objectors may raise. Experiences in 1995 showed that the consideration and processing of applications, although handled expeditiously by officials, was sometimes at odds with companies' desires to have Drought Orders in place as rapidly as possible in order to arrest fast-deteriorating situations. While more recent applications have in general not given rise to the same tensions, it is the Government's intention to review the process by which Drought Orders are applied for and considered, in order to establish whether there is scope for improving that process. Clearly, one factor which will need consideration is the timeliness with which companies themselves identify and act upon a need to apply for Drought Orders.

Drinking water quality

10.23 Water supplies need to be maintained secure in terms not only of quantity but also of quality. The overall quality of drinking water in England and Wales is very high – 99.5% of the 3.1 million tests carried out in 1995 demonstrated compliance with the standards (DoE, 1996). The Drinking Water Inspectorate will continue its technical assessments and checks of companies' quality monitoring results. It will take enforcement action if any of the quality standards are breached or if any of the other regulatory requirements concerning monitoring, water treatment or the provision of information are not met.

Availability of Water Resources and Security of Supply

10.24 The Regulations (Statutory Instruments, 1989) lay down standards not only for water entering and in public water supply, but also for the quality of raw water abstracted from surface water sources according to the type of treatment to be applied. The Regulations also provide for control over the use of water treatment processes and over the use of products and substances which come into contact with drinking water. By these means, the Regulations provide a mechanism for ensuring that drinking water quality is not compromised either by the quality of the water source or by the use of an inappropriate treatment process. The Drinking Water Inspectorate will continue its vigilance in these respects.

Supply failure: compensation

10.25 If security of supply is inadequate, customers might be subject to hosepipe bans, restrictions on non-essential use of water, water pressure reductions or rota cuts[15]. However, they currently have no statutory entitlement to compensation. Under section 79 of the Water Resources Act 1991, water undertakers have no liability for losses or damage sustained by their customers as a result of the implementation of Drought Orders.

10.26 As a result of such difficulties that summer, in September 1995 the Secretary of State asked the Director General of Water Services for advice on compensation issues. The Director issued a consultation paper in December 1995 and published his recommendations to the Secretary of State in May 1996 (Ofwat, 1996c). These recommend the payment of compensation to household and business customers who experience interruptions to their supply as a result of emergency restrictions, and to customers who are affected by low water pressure. The Secretary of State welcomed these proposals and has announced his intention to introduce legislation as necessary when Parliamentary time allows. Water companies are of course already able to establish compensation schemes of their own to cover these circumstances. Some have already done so.

---

15 Although the first three of these difficulties were experienced to varying degrees by customers in certain areas during 1995, it must be emphasised that **no consumers were subjected to rota cuts.**

Future Need for New Water Resources

Assessment of future needs

11.1 Earlier sections of this paper have reviewed some of the main factors which influence the availability of water and demand on public water supply systems. These include the reliable yield from existing resources, losses in distribution, trends in unconstrained demand, the scope for influencing that demand through volumetric charging and by other means, and choices over the level of security of supply to be achieved. This section looks at the possible balance between supply and demand, the relevance of the earlier conclusions to reassessing that balance, and the rôle of the companies and regulators in planning how an appropriate balance is to be maintained in future years.

11.2 The NRA publication "Water: Nature's Precious Resource" (NRA, 1994) identified a number of local and strategic resource options for meeting increased demand on water resources and gave an indication of the likely dates by which the various strategic options would be needed in the face of the three demand scenarios featured in the report (see paragraph 10.4). This exercise was based on 1991 data and also assumed that a range of local resource development options would be taken up first.

11.3 A further assessment of the likely need for new strategic resources was carried out by the NRA (on the eve of its incorporation into the Environment Agency) for the purposes of this review, based on the approach previously used, but with additional data and other information supplied by water companies to Ofwat. It is important to note that this work (NRA, 1996) did not seek to update the national strategy contained in "Water, Nature's Precious Resource", but rather to assess what impact different basic assumptions could have on that strategy.

11.4 Unlike the earlier work, the new assessment considers the effect of prolonged peak demands upon resources and takes into account the possibility of a reduction in reliable yields resulting from changed design standards. It constructs four scenarios against combinations of demand increase and resource yield decrease. These are summarised in Table 11. The first three take as their basis a demand forecast which assumes savings from leakage control and increased penetration of metering, but the fourth assumes that these savings are not in fact achieved. Although the third and fourth scenarios make allowance for hot summer droughts of the kind experienced in 1995, the scenarios are not based on formal climate change studies.

11.5 Under the most pessimistic scenario, the outcome is very similar in its resource development consequences to the "High" scenario featured in the earlier NRA work (NRA, 1994) and could lead to the need for seven strategic schemes within the period 1996 to 2021. Under the most optimistic scenario there would be no need for any significant resource development in the period to the year 2015.

11.6 It must be appreciated that the scenario approaches outlined above provide indications of what might come to pass in respect of resources if the assumptions on which they are founded are realised. They should not be construed as presenting a formal action plan for development of new resources, although "Water: Nature's Precious Resource", in presenting an environmentally sustainable water resources development strategy[16], outlines the resource development schemes which might be needed under its scenarios and which might be most acceptable when account is taken of their associated environmental considerations. The NRA also prepared strategies for sustainable water resources management for each of its regions, building upon the foundation of the strategy for England and Wales as whole contained in "Water: Nature's Precious Resource". All these strategies should be taken forward and revised as appropriate by the Environment Agency, necessarily in consultation with the water companies.

11.7 Water companies should take full account of the issues and information mentioned in the previous paragraphs in drawing up and modifying their own plans for water resource development. However, the Environment Agency has recently drawn attention to the desirability of ensuring that each company's resource plans are fully and regularly communicated to the Agency so that any concerns about a company's interpretation of its situation or about the environmental acceptability of its planned developments can be identified and resolved. The Government agrees that it is important that the Agency should have full access to companies' plans to enable it to discharge effectively its own duties in relation to water resource manage-

Future Need for New Water Resources

ment and is considering whether further powers for the Agency in this area are necessary (see paragraph 3.23).

Influencing future needs

11.8 The scenario approaches described above are founded on the entirely reasonable expectation that the actual water resources position which develops over a period of time in a particular area can be influenced to a significant extent by water companies. This paper has highlighted the key rôle of:

- promotion of increased efficiency of water use;
- innovative approaches to charging for water; and
- reduction of leakage

in managing demand for public water supplies. However, the actual extent to which demand management can defer or remove the need for new water resource developments within a given time horizon will depend on local considerations which may vary between and within companies. It will also depend on the relative costs of demand management and resource development. In making this assessment, companies will need to take into account the full range of costs and benefits of differing combinations of these approaches, in line with the principles of sustainable development.

11.9 New resource development needs will also be determined in part by water companies entering into dialogue with their customers on the level of security of water supply which they desire, as discussed in paragraph 10.16. This process will provide an essential component in making the case for new resources.

11.10 A case for new resources will be compelling only if there is insufficient scope for deployment of existing resources to meet properly-managed demand. In considering this point, companies will naturally look first at options fully within their own control, but should then move on to consider alternatives which would involve actions by others.

11.11 As some companies' responses to the 1995 drought showed, provision of new raw or treated water mains to enable transfers of water within companies' boundaries can improve deployment of resources. Reinstatement of abstraction points which have previously been abandoned on narrow grounds of operating cost may prove to be cost effective when assessed against costs of developing new resources. It may also be possible for some companies to take action to enhance the recharging of water resource systems – the large artificial recharge scheme for the North East London aquifer provides a good example of this.

Developing use of existing resources

11.12 Currently developed water resources owe their origin mainly to geography – the geography both of the water resources themselves and also of the demand centres which for which they were developed. Although their origins were also influenced by the structure of the water industry in past times, their continued availability to meet present and future demands ought not to be constrained by boundaries of ownership.

11.13 Indeed, several major water resource developments in previous decades were conceived and implemented on a co-operative basis between separate water companies or water boards. This history is represented in the present existence in England and Wales of more than 25 agreements between companies for bulk transfers of raw water, ranging in size from less than 1 Ml/d to 360 Ml/d. There is no legal or procedural obstacle to companies freely making agreements amongst themselves for new bulk transfers of water where present organisational boundaries and demand within them do not fully coincide with existing resource availability.

11.14 Moreover, the legislation provides a mechanism whereby a company wishing to secure a bulk transfer from a reluctant donor can apply for the Director General of Water Services to make an order to that effect if he is satisfied that the donor company is able to sustain the supply. This mechanism is more fully described in paragraph 31 of Annex B. The Environment Agency has recently stated its view that there is a need to ensure that these powers are effective and the Government is considering this matter (see paragraph 3.23). However, water companies should consider carefully the scope the present powers might offer for the relief of water resource difficulties which, on independent examination, may prove to be more organisational than geographic in nature.

11.15 Access to existing developed water resources is governed by licensing. As described in paragraph 32ff of Annex B, water abstractions have to be licensed by the Environment Agency. Licences are granted to the occupier of the land from which the abstraction is made and pass to successive occupiers provided they give the Agency notification of the change. So, whether by outright sale or by rental of the land, water companies can, by negotiation either between themselves or with other licence holders, redistribute existing water resources within the present organisational arrangements of the industry.

11.16 If transfer of licences in this way is not amenable to negotiation between the parties who would need to be involved, the powers of licence revocation or modification (see paragraph 34 of Annex B) could be brought to bear by the Environment Agency so as to enable access to existing water resources by a new abstractor. However, unless the existing licence holder has voluntarily sought revocation, or has failed to abstract any water for at least seven years, compensation is payable and would need to figure in any overall appraisal of options.

11.17 The Environment Agency has recently expressed the view that powers in respect of abstraction licence transfers need to provide an effective means of redistributing water resources where necessary. The Government is considering this point. The Government attaches importance to ensuring that the right price signals are in place to provide companies with appropriate incentives to encourage the efficient distribution of water resources. It is therefore examining the possibility of introducing tradeable permits for water abstraction as a means of encouraging redistribution according to value, together with more general options for making water abstraction charges more reflective of environmental costs and overall value of the resource. It will seek to publish a consultation paper on economic instruments in relation to water abstraction by early 1997.

11.18 Greater local inter-linkage of resources or supply systems gives greater flexibility to meet local shortages from other water sources in a company's area. Its value may be limited if the shortage of rainfall is general in the company's area and all sources are under pressure. Long-distance inter-linkage enables water to be carried from areas where it is usually plentiful to areas that are likely otherwise to be under frequent pressure of demand. In both cases, but particularly in the latter, there may be significant environmental problems to be solved.

11.19 Inter-linkage has been developing gradually over the last two decades, in the form of company trunk mains, co-operative schemes, and transfer schemes like that from the lower reaches of the Great Ouse near the Wash to the low-rainfall, highly urbanised areas of Essex. Long-distance inter-linkage has long been in place between Wales and the West Midlands and South East Lancashire, and between the Lake District and Lancashire. The latter systems were extended locally last winter to increase flexibility of supply to the west-ern Pennine towns. Further long-distance schemes are under consideration, for example, to enable Kielder water to be supplied to Yorkshire, and to allow water to reach the lower Thames from central Wales.

11.20 In this way, the water "grid" or more properly "grids" are being extended according to need and provided any significant environmental difficulties can be overcome. It is misleading, however, to think in terms of a "national grid" analogous to those for electricity and gas: the density and more variable characteristics of water mean that both the practicalities and economics are different.

Development of new resources

11.21 Even with full use of the various means, described above, by which it can be deferred, detailed assessments of the balance between existing resources and future demand may still show the need for development of new water resources.

11.22 Water companies have the duty to develop and maintain an efficient and economical system of water supply within their areas (see paragraph 3.5). Compliance with this duty must necessarily involve them in planning new water resource development in order to maintain efficiency.

11.23 If there were any doubt in the matter, section 6(2) of the Environment Act 1995 makes it plain that water companies' obligations in this respect are not relieved by the duty upon the Environment Agency in respect of augmentation of water supplies (see paragraph 3.13f). However, that same statutory provision also signals the need for the Environment Agency and water companies to work together in water resource development. Moreover, just as in times past major new resources were developed by water companies or water boards acting co-operatively, so might the present water industry consider the scope for joint ventures in promoting strategic water resource schemes.

11.24 Promotion of new resources is thus a matter for water companies and the Environment Agency in view of their specific duties in respect of water resources, but the Director General of Water Services has a major rôle to play in view of his responsibilities on behalf of customers and in respect of water company financing (see paragraph 1f of Annex B). That rôle encompasses enforcement action if, in consultation with the Environment Agency, the Director were to conclude that a water company, in failing to promote new re-

Future Need for New Water Resources

source development, was failing in its duty to develop an efficient system of water supply (see paragraph 5 of Annex B).

11.25 The Government's view is therefore that, as the primary responsibility for maintaining water supplies rests with the water companies, so it is the responsibility of those companies, either individually or co-operatively with one another and with full involvement of – or if necessary through enforcement by – the regulators, to draw up plans for the timely development of new resources if the projected demand for water in particular areas cannot be reasonably or reliably managed to remain within the capacity of all the existing resources which could supply those areas.

11.26 The costs of new resources, and more generally of effective management of water resources and supply, fall to be considered by the Director General of Water Services within the general financial framework of the industry. This includes a duty on the Director to ensure that water companies can finance their functions. Whether a particular scheme calls for an increase in revenue will depend on the overall financial position and efficiency of the company as assessed by the Director.

11.27 In considering the nature and timing of such development, significant allowance has to be made for the planning process, which is likely to be protracted in view of the imperative to consider carefully the environmental impact of any new scheme, and the margin of uncertainty in the particular case. Moreover, there has to be a clear strategy for maintaining supplies in the meantime at an acceptable level of security without resort to drought orders or other measures which may prove environmentally controversial (see paragraph 10.21).

11.28 There is within the water industry a body of relatively recent experience in bringing forward plans for new resource development. A review of this collective experience by water companies which might wish now

to develop new resources may illuminate ways in which future schemes may be designed and promoted from the outset so as best to take account of the environmental concerns which would feature prominently in the planning process.

11.29 The precise timing of new resource development should work back from the date by which it would need to be in service to meet the demands which are projected to make it necessary. Challenging but realistic assessment of the extent to which demand can be managed needs to inform the projections of demand – there will be no merit in timing development on the basis of demand management targets which are not, for whatever reason, subsequently met. Nor will there be merit in over-optimistic predictions of the time within which new resources can be brought into service. There has to be a reasonable safety margin.

11.30 It follows from this, and from the material presented earlier in this paper, that the balance between present and projected demand for water supplies and the reliable yield of existing water resources must be kept under continuous review, taking into account new data on either side of the balance, together with new information on factors, such as climate change, which could affect the balance in future.

11.31 The Government's view is that planning of new resource development for areas where the existing resources are most finely balanced (at the customers' desired level of security) against projected demand increases should proceed in parallel with the continued implementation of all the measures and mechanisms which are available to meet that demand from already-developed resources, and against the background of a continuous review of that balance. That planning and the related decisions should take into account the inherent uncertainties referred to in paragraph 2.16.

12.1 This paper has identified needs for the following actions:

(a) modifications to the legal framework if it were to emerge that the mechanisms it provides for maintaining excellent standards of service while protecting the environment could be further refined:

- ◆ **action** by **Government** at the earliest opportunity (see paragraph 3.23*ff*);

(b) prepare – by means of up to date consistent assumptions and methodology – fresh estimates of the current reliable yields of each discrete water resource system, taking into account its current operation and recent hydrometric data:

- ◆ **action** by individual **water companies** with co-ordination by the **Environment Agency** and publication of resulting information by the Agency by the end of 1997 (see paragraph 4.10);

(c) test the fresh estimates of current reliable yields against climate change scenarios:

- ◆ **action** to be led by the **Environment Agency**, in full consultation with the water companies and in close contact with Government and centres of excellence on climate change studies (see paragraph 4.17*ff*);

(d) establish further detailed measurements of how water is used within households in order better to forecast overall demand for water:

- ◆ **action** by each individual **water company**, with a view to all having commenced data gathering by the end of 1997 (see paragraph 5.18*ff*);

(e) conduct further studies of the implications for demand on public water supplies of climate change scenarios:

- ◆ **action** led by **water companies**, probably through a co-operative approach and in any case in close collaboration with centres of excellence, to progress at the fastest possible rate (see paragraph 5.22*ff*).

(f) continue the development and marketing of water-efficient and water saving equipment and fittings:

- ◆ **action** by **manufacturers**, with appropriate input from water companies and consumer organisations (see paragraph 7.4*ff*);

(g) incorporation of revised regulatory requirements in respect of water conservation in new Regulations:

- ◆ **action** by **Government** in the light of advice from the Water Regulations Advisory Committee, in the expectation that new Regulations will be in force by late 1998 (see paragraph 7.11);

(h) further efforts to promote water conservation, drawing on a range of short and longer-term options to suit local circumstances and recognising the added incentive for water conservation which charging by volume provides:

- ◆ **action** by **water companies**, in the light of their statutory duty to promote the efficient use of water by their customers as monitored by the **Office of Water Services**, but not precluding further developments and initiatives by companies according to particular circumstances or opportunities within their areas (see paragraph 7.16ff);
- ◆ **action** also by **consumers**, who will need to be made aware of the importance of water conservation to themselves and to their environment so as to be persuaded of the need to respond constructively to water efficiency initiatives (see, *inter alia*, paragraph 7.15);
- ◆ **action** by **Government**, drawing upon techniques used in the implementation of its environmental management and energy efficiency policies (see paragraph 7.24);

(i) further extension of charging for water by metered volume used:

- ◆ **action** by **water companies**, with especial urgency in relation to customers with an actual or potential high use of water (see paragraphs 8.2 and 8.15);

(j) consideration of more sophisticated tariff structures as means of optimising demand management through water charges:

- ◆ **action** by individual **water companies**, with rapid progress consistent with the need for consultation with customers and the Office of Water Services (see paragraph 8.23);

Actions

(k) build on existing work on leakage and:

    i) apply on a consistent basis methods for estimating and expressing leakage levels;

    ii) assess economic levels of leakage, taking full account of environmental costs; and

    iii) adopt clear programmes and targets for leakage control to economic levels, with rigorous procedures for assessment and reporting of progress in meeting them:

◆ **action** by **water companies**, with monitoring and reporting by the **Office of Water Services** (see paragraph 9.16ff);

(l) dialogue between water companies and their customers on the balance to be struck between higher security of supply and higher costs:

◆ **action** by each individual **water company** with its customers as represented through the Customer Service Committees of the Office of Water Services and other organisations able to represent the views of consumer groups in particular areas, within a timescale which would depend on the Director's intentions for the timing of his next review (see paragraph 10.6ff);

(m) review the process for Drought Order applications:

◆ **action** by the **Government**, with input from water companies (see paragraph 10.22);

(n) continued monitoring of compliance with regulatory standards for drinking water quality and water treatment:

◆ **action** by the **Drinking Water Inspectorate** (see paragraph 10.23f);

(o) revise, as necessary, national and regional water resources strategies:

◆ **action** by **the Environment Agency**, in full consultation with the water companies (see paragraph 11.6);

(p) consultation on economic instruments applied to water abstraction:

◆ **action** by the **Government** (see paragraph 11.17);

(q) draw up plans for the timely development of new resources if the projected demand for water in particular areas cannot be reasonably or reliably managed to remain within the capacity of all the existing resources which could supply those areas:

◆ **action** by **water companies**, either individually or co-operatively with one another and with the full involvement of the **regulators**, to proceed in parallel with the continued implementation of all the measures and mechanisms which are available to meet that demand from already-developed resources, and against the background of a continuous review of that balance (see paragraph 11.25ff); and

(r) implement compensation arrangements for customers affected by water supply interruptions or low water pressure:

◆ legislative **action** by the **Government,** with **water companies** encouraged to establish their own compensation schemes in the meantime (see paragraph 10.26).

12.2 Thus, grouping each of these actions for each organisation, the **Government** will:

(a) bring forward modifications to the legal framework if scope for further refinement were to emerge (although it is satisfied that the basic framework is sound);

(b) continue to promote research into climate change;

(c) revise regulatory requirements in respect of water conservation in the light of advice from its Water Regulations Advisory Committee;

(d) draw on its experience in promoting environmental management and energy efficiency to assist the relevant organisations in the promotion of efficient use of water;

(e) review the process for Drought Order applications;

(f) consult on the use of economic instruments in relation to water abstraction; and

(g) introduce legislation as necessary for compensation arrangements for customers affected by supply interruptions or low pressure.

12.3 The **Environment Agency** should:

(a) co-ordinate the fresh estimating of the reliable yields of water resource systems and publish the resulting information;

(b) lead the testing of those estimates against climate change scenarios;

(c) revise, as necessary, its national and regional water resources strategies in consultation with the water companies; and

(d) be fully involved with water companies' new resource development plans.

Actions

12.4 The **Office of Water Services** should:

(a) monitor and as necessary enforce water companies' performance of their duty to promote the efficient use of water by their customers;

(b) monitor, report and, as necessary, take further action on leakage control;

(c) be fully involved with water companies' new resource development plans; and

(d) consider the financial implications of new water resources and supply schemes as necessary in the course of its normal price regulation activities.

12.5 The **Drinking Water Inspectorate** will:

(a) check that all water supplies are monitored in accordance with and meet regulatory quality requirements;

(b) check that water treatment processes comply with regulatory requirements; and

(c) take enforcement action if regulatory requirements are not met.

12.6 **Water companies** should:

(a) prepare fresh estimates of the reliable yields of water resource systems;

(b) establish further detailed measurements of household water use;

(c) conduct further studies of the implications of climate change on demand for water;

(d) extend the penetration of metering;

(e) develop more sophisticated tariff structures;

(f) increase efforts to promote water conservation;

(g) improve leakage measurement, control and reporting;

(h) enter into dialogue with customers about security of supply; and

(i) draw up plans for timely development of new water resources where demand cannot be managed to remain within existing resource capability.

12.7 **Manufacturers of water-using equipment and fittings** should:

(a) continue to develop and market energetically more water-efficient products; and

(b) continue innovation in the field of water recycling systems.

12.8 **Water consumers** should:

(a) take full notice of information from water companies and other organisations on the need for water efficiency and how to achieve it;

(b) recognise the environmental significance of water conservation; and

(c) take every opportunity to use water wisely.

12.9 These assignments should not be regarded as implying fixed territories into which other bodies should not intrude. Government, regulators and the water companies all need to continue to work together in co-ordination to ensure the effectiveness of their combined actions so as to maintain entirely satisfactory water supplies. Nor should the rôle of the wider water industry – researchers, manufactures, suppliers and consultants – be overlooked. Professional bodies should see considerable scope for promoting discussion and disseminating developments in the various action areas. Other organisations should encourage from their various distinctive viewpoints.

12.10 Nevertheless, under the legal and regulatory framework for water resources and supply arrangements, the various actions are, in the final analysis, clearly the primary concern of particular organisations. Many of the actions identified in this paper fall to the water companies. This is as it should be; they should have the knowledge, skills, customer awareness and financial resources with which to address the solemn responsibility which their appointment as water undertakers gives them – the duty to maintain public water supplies both now and in the longer term.

References

CCIRG, 1996. *Review of the Potential Effects of Climate Change in the United Kingdom*. HMSO, London, July 1996.

DoE, 1992a. *Planning Policy Guidance: Development Plans and Regional Planning Guidance*. Department of the Environment, February 1992.

DoE, 1992b. *Using Water Wisely – A Consultation Paper*. Department of the Environment and Welsh Office, July 1992.

DoE, 1995a. *Water Conservation – Government Action*. Department of the Environment and Welsh Office, August 1995.

DoE, 1995b. *Replacing the Water Byelaws – A Consultation Paper*. Department of the Environment and Welsh Office, January 1995.

DoE, 1996. *Drinking Water 1995 – A report by the Chief Inspector, Drinking Water Inspectorate*. Department of the Environment and Welsh Office, June 1996.

Edwards, K., and Martin, L., 1995. *A Methodology for Surveying Domestic Water Consumption*. Journal of the Chartered Institution of Water and Environmental Management, 9(5), 477-488.

Environment Committee, 1996. *Water Conservation and Supply – Interim Report*. House of Commons Environment Committee, 24 July 1996.

Environmental Technology Best Practice Programme, 1996. *Saving money through waste minimisation: reducing water use*. GG26 Guide (first printed March 1996)

Herbertson, P.W., and Howarth, D.A., 1996. *Approaches to water conservation and demand management in the UK, Europe and the USA*. In "Supply and Demand – a Fragile Balance", Chartered Institution of Water and Environmental Management, March 1996.

Herrington, P., 1996a. *Climate Change and the Demand for Water*. HMSO, London, 1996.

Herrington, P., 1996b. *Pricing Water Properly*. University of Leicester Discussion Paper, 1996.

IPCC, 1996. *Climate Change 1995 – The Science of Climate Change: Summary for Policymakers and Technical Summary of the Working Group I Report*. Intergovernmental Panel on Climate Change 1996.

Marsh, T.J., and Turton, P.S., 1996. *The 1995 drought – a water resources perspective*. "Weather", February 1996.

National Metering Trials Working Group, 1993. *Water Metering Trials – Final Report*. Water Services Association, Water Companies Association, Office of Water Services, WRc and Department of the Environment, 1993.

NRA, 1994. *Water: Nature's Precious Resource*. National Rivers Authority, March 1994.

NRA, 1995a. *Surface Water Yield Assessment*. R&D Note 313. National Rivers Authority, 1995.

NRA, 1995b. *Domestic Consumption Monitoring Survey – DMC Project 5*. National Rivers Authority, July 1995.

NRA, 1995c. *Saving Water*. National Rivers Authority, September 1995.

NRA, 1996. Unpublished report to the Department of the Environment.

NWC, 1980. *Technical Working Group on Waste of Water. Leakage Control Policy and Practice. Standing Technical Committee Report No 26*. National Water Council, 1980.

OECD, 1987. *Pricing of Water Services*. Organisation for Economic Co-operation and Development, Paris, 1987.

Ofwat, 1994. *Future Levels of Demand and Supply for Water. Ofwat Occasional Paper 1*. Office of Water Services, November 1994.

Ofwat, 1996a. *Leakage of water in England and Wales*. Office of Water Services, May 1996.

Ofwat, 1996b. *Report on recent patterns of demand for water in England and Wales*. Office of Water Services, May 1996.

Ofwat, 1996c. *Recommendations to the Secretary of State for the Environment and the Secretary of State for Wales on compensation issues raised by the 1995 drought*. Office of Water Services, May 1996.

Parry, M, and Duncan, R, 1995. *The Economic Implications of Climate Change in Britain*. Earthscan Publications, London.

Statutory Instruments, 1989. *The Water Supply (Water Quality) Regulations 1989*. 1989 No. 1147, as amended by 1989 No. 1384 and 1991 No. 1837.

UK Water Industry, 1994. *Managing Leakage*. WRc plc/Water Services Association/Water Companies Association, 1994.

Water Services Association, 1995. *Waterfacts 1995*.

WS Atkins, 1992. *The Social Impact of Water Metering*. (An investigation jointly funded by the Department of the Environment and the Office of Water Services). WS Atkins Planning and Management Consultants, August 1992.

Tables

Table 1: minimum five-month rainfall totals for England and Wales, 1850 – 1995.

Rank	Cumulative rainfall (mm)	Percentage of average (a)	End month	Year
1	149	43.1	08	1995
2	155	44.8	08	1976
3	159	50.7	06	1921
4	184	58.7	06	1938
5	185	59.0	06	1929
6	186	59.3	06	1887
7	187	52.5	04	1854
8	188	57.6	07	1870
9	191	51.2	09	1959

(a) The averages are not in the same rank order because they are different for different end dates.

Table 2: standard period average rainfall (mm) for England and Wales.

| Month | Period | | |
	1916-1950	1941-1970	1961-1990
January	92	86	88
February	66	65	63
March	57	59	72
April	60	58	60
May	63	67	64
June	55	61	65
July	79	73	62
August	81	90	76
September	76	83	77
October	92	83	85
November	95	97	90
December	88	90	94
ANNUAL AVERAGE	904	912	895

Table 3: water put into public supply in England and Wales – annual averages in Megalitres per day (Ml/d).

| Year | Unmetered | Average, Ml/d | |
		Metered	TOTAL
1974/75	9,555	4,801	14,356
1975/76	9,907	4,668	14,575
1976/77	9,519	4,359	13,878
1977/78	9,961	4,211	14,172
1978/79	10,407	4,352	14,759
1979/80	10,961	4,490	15,451
1980/81	11,083	4,247	15,330
1981/82	11,224	4,029	15,253
1982/83	11,548	4,106	15,654
1983/84	11,842	3,996	15,838
1984/85	11,956	3,990	15,946
1985/86	12,036	3,965	16,001
1986/87	12,195	4,088	16,283
1987/88	12,216	4,059	16,275
1988/89	12,177	4,114	16,291
1989/90	12,424	4,135	16,559
1990/91	12,549	4,256	16,805
1991/92	12,399	4,258	16,657
1992/93	11,669	4,457	16,126
1993/94	11,999	4,034	16,033
1994/95	12,350	4,139	16,489

Tables

Table 4: water put into public supply in former water authority regions – annual averages in Megalitres per day (Ml/d).

Region	1975	1994/95	% change
Anglian	1,450	1,743	20
North West	2,450	2,455	<1
Northumbrian	960	1,071	12
Severn Trent	2,180	2,504	15
South West	380	476	25
Southern	1,090	1,204	10
Thames	3,360	3,884	16
Welsh	1,130	1,244	10
Wessex	710	926	30
Yorkshire	1,280	1,508	14
ENGLAND and WALES	14,990	17,015	14

Table 5: water put into public supply in former water authority regions – annual averages in Megalitres per day (Ml/d).

Region	1990/91	1991/92	1992/93	1993/94	1994/95
Anglian	1,843	1,758	1,696	1,695	1,743
North West	2,485	2,591	2,556	2,487	2,455
Northumbrian	1,075	1,068	1,049	1,074	1,071
Severn Trent	2,421	2,409	2,414	2,433	2,504
South West	498	500	485	477	476
Southern	1,303	1,231	1,193	1,176	1,204
Thames	4,105	3,983	3,800	3,740	3,884
Welsh	1,273	1,273	1,250	1,238	1,244
Wessex	907	885	873	880	926
Yorkshire	1,472	1,506	1,469	1,476	1,508

Table 6: estimated effect of domestic metering in trials in England, 1988-92.

Area	Change in water consumption	Tariff
Bristol	+1.6%	Flat-rate
East Worcester	-17.2%	Seasonal
Mid Southern	-7.3%	Flat-rate
Northumbrian	-16.1%	Declining block
Southern	-12.3%	Seasonal
Thames	-10.9%	Increasing block
Three Valleys	-8.4%	Peak-rate/flat-rate
Wessex (Broadstone)	-12.4%	Peak-rate
Wessex (Turlin Moor)	-10.5%	Flat-rate
Yorkshire	-13.7%	Increasing block
SMALL SCALE SITES (average of the above)	-10.8%	—
Isle of Wight (LARGE SCALE)	-21.3%	Increasing block

Tables

Table 7: average regional public water supply surpluses.

This table shows the annual average surplus as a percentage of the annual average demand in each of the eight regions into which the NRA was latterly organised.

Region	1991	1992	1993	1994	1995
Anglian	26	27	32	29	22
North East(a)	42	48	50	49	46
North West	9	10	11	14	14
Severn Trent	13	14	14	13	17
South West(b)	18	19	20	21	11
Southern	24	24	28	29	21
Thames	9	9	14	16	5
Welsh	26	30	32	34	25

(a)   the former Northumbrian and Yorkshire NRA regions.
(b)   the former South West and Wessex NRA regions.

Table 8: assumptions used for each of the three demand scenarios for 2021 considered in "Water: Nature's Precious Resource" (NRA, 1994).

Assumptions	Scenario		
	High	Medium	Low
1. Growth of per capita consumption by compound annual rate of 1%. Per capita figures are constrained to a maximum of 189 l/h/d. Existing per capita consumption from returns to Ofwat for 1992.	◆		
2. Growth of per capita consumption by compound annual percentage rates derived from special study. Per capita figures are constrained to a maximum of 180 l/h/d. Existing per capita consumption from returns to Ofwat for 1992.		◆	◆
3. Growth in metered and unmetered non-household consumption by compound annual rate of 0.75% (for all water supply companies).	◆		
4. As assumption 3, but rate of 0.50%.		◆	
5. No growth in metered and unmetered non-household consumption above 1991 levels.			◆
6. No increase in the proportion of domestic properties subject to metering above 1991 levels (for all companies). Existing metered properties per capita consumption not reduced by 10% in recognition of the uncertainty associated with such a reduction. Assumed leakage reductions of 30 l/prop/d to account for decreased supply pipe leakage in existing metered properties.	◆		
7. For companies in Anglian, Severn Trent, Southern, Thames and Wessex regions 15% of domestic properties will have meters by 2021 (starting in 1996 with equal phasing each year) leading to a 10% reduction in per capita consumption and a reduction in water losses of 30 l/prop/d to account for reduced supply pipe leakage in metered properties. Assumption 6 applies in other regions.		◆	
8. As assumption 7, but with metering in 30% of the properties in the specified regions by 2006.			◆
9. Leakage per property held at 1991 levels to simulate the effect of no improvements being made to reduce leakage levels. However, if existing leakage is above 290 l/prop/d then it is reduced to this level at an annual rate of 10l/prop/d.	◆		
10. Leakage targets achieved effecting a reduction in total treated water losses to 140 l/prop/d in Anglian, Severn Trent,Southern, Thames and Wessex regions and 220 l/prop/d in other regions.		◆	
11. As assumption 10, but with water losses of 120 and 200 l/prop/d in the respective cases.			◆

Tables

Table 9: water demand predicted under the three scenarios considered in "Water: Nature's Precious Resource" (NRA, 1994).

Region	Water into supply, 1994/95	Predicted demand (Ml/d) in 2021 under scenario:		
		High	Medium	Low
Anglian	1,743	2,372	2,206	2,039
North West	2,455	2,872	2,493	2,329
Northumbrian	1,071	1,003	944	892
Severn Trent	2,504	3,098	2,702	2,477
South West	476	715	632	594
Southern	1,204	1,603	1,406	1,298
Thames	3,884	5,093	4,238	3,892
Welsh	1,244	1,360	1,190	1,117
Wessex	926	1,155	999	924
Yorkshire	1,508	1,858	1,621	1,512
TOTAL	17,015	21,129	18,431	17,074

Table 10: strategic water resources deficits predicted under the three scenarios considered in "Water: Nature's Precious Resource" (NRA, 1994).

Region	Deficit (Ml/d) in 2021 under scenario:		
	High	Medium	Low
Anglian	128	72	0
North West	0	0	0
Northumbrian	0	0	0
Severn Trent	252	4	0
South West	0	0	0
Southern	0	0	0
Thames	629	66	5
Welsh	0	0	0
Wessex	84	0	0
Yorkshire	0	0	0
TOTAL	1,093	142	5

Table 11: scenarios for assessing the need for new resources (NRA, 1996).

Scenario A uses:

- demand forecasts obtained in confidence from the Strategic Business Plans submitted to Ofwat by companies in 1994; and
- reliable yields of existing water resources as used for "Water: Nature's Precious Resource" (NRA, 1994).

Scenario B is as Scenario A, except that reliable yields are reduced by 5% throughout to represent a possible outcome of yield reassessment.

Scenario C is as Scenario B, except that demand forecasts are increased by 10% to allow for demand in hot summer droughts.

Scenario D is as Scenario C, except that it assumes that companies' 1994 forecasts of demand savings from leakage reduction and extension of metering will not be achieved.

Annex A

ORGANISATIONS RESPONDING TO THE INVITATION TO CONTRIBUTE TO THE REVIEW

Association of County Councils

Association of District Councils

The Association of Manufacturers of Domestic Electrical Appliances

British Institute of Architectural Technologists

Canterbury Friends of the Earth

The Chartered Institute of Building

The Chartered Institution of Building Services Engineers

The Chartered Institution of Water and Environmental Management

Confederation of British Industry

The Council for the Protection of Rural England

The Council of Welsh Districts

Country Landowners Association

The Institute of Building Control

The Institute of Plumbing

Natural Environment Research Council

Royal Horticultural Society

The Royal Society for the Protection of Birds

The Royal Town Planning Institute

Save the Children

Society of British Water Industries

Water Training International

WRc PLC

THE LEGAL AND REGULATORY FRAMEWORK IN RESPECT OF WATER RESOURCES AND SUPPLY ARRANGEMENTS

The Director General of Water Services

1   The Director General of Water Services ("the Director") is appointed by the Secretary of State under section 1 of the Water Industry Act 1991. The Director or, as the case may be, the Secretary of State is required by section 2(2) of that Act to exercise his powers and duties relating to the regulation of water undertakers in 'the manner which he considers is best calculated to secure that the functions of a water undertaker… are properly carried out' and, without prejudice to that generality, to secure that water undertakers are 'able (in particular, by securing reasonable returns on their capital) to finance the proper carrying out of [their] functions'.

2   Subject to these primary requirements, the Director or, as the case may be, the Secretary of State, is also required, amongst other provisions of section 2(3) of the Act, to:

(a)   ensure that customers' interests are protected in respect of charges, and in particular that customers in rural areas are protected and that there is no undue preference or discrimination in the fixing of charges;

(b)   ensure that customers interests are protected in respect of the terms on which services are provided and the quality of those services;

(c)   promote economy and efficiency on the part of water undertakers carrying out their functions; and to

(d)   facilitate effective competition between companies holding or seeking appointments as water undertakers.

3   The powers and duties of the Director range widely in respect of the activities and standards of performance of water undertakers. Beyond the powers of the Secretary of State to appoint, remove and remunerate him, the Director operates independently, except to the extent that the exercise of his duties might lead him to recommend to the Secretary of State consideration of legislative changes, or in respect of certain duties on water undertakers for which only the Secretary of State can initiate enforcement action. The Director is required, by section 193 of the Water Industry Act 1991, to report to the Secretary of State on his activities each year.

The Environment Agency

4   The Environment Agency is a body corporate whose members are appointed under section 1 of the Environment Act 1995. Section 4 of the Act gives it the principal aim in discharging its functions so to protect or enhance the environment, taken as a whole, as to make contribution to towards attaining the objective of achieving sustainable development, under the guidance of Ministers. Under section 6(2), Ministers have the power to give the Agency directions of a general or specific character with respect to the carrying out of its functions. Ministers may also, under section 51 of the Environment Act 1995, require the Agency to furnish such information relating to its responsibilities and conduct of its functions as they may reasonably require. The Agency is required, by section 52 of the Environment Act 1995, to provide an annual report on its activities to Ministers.

General duty to maintain water supply systems

5   The statutory responsibility for public water supplies rests with companies which are appointed as water undertakers under section 6 of the Water Industry Act 1991. Under section 37 of that Act, a water undertaker has the duty 'to develop and maintain an efficient and economical system of water supply within its area and to ensure that all such arrangements have been made…

(a)   for providing supplies of water to premises in that area and for making such supplies available to persons who demand them; and

(b)   for maintaining, improving and extending the water undertaker's water mains and other pipes,

as are necessary for securing that the undertaker is and continues to be able to meet its obligations under [Part III of the Act on water supply]'.

6   This duty of is enforceable under section 18 of the Water Industry Act 1991 by the Secretary of State or the Director. Sections 38 and 39 of that Act empower the Secretary of State, on the recommendation of the Director and after the latter's consultation with water undertakers, to establish by regulations overall standards of performance to facilitate assessment of compliance with this duty. If these were not met, the breach would amount to a breach of section 37. To date, regulations have been made under these provisions only in respect of certain standards of customer service required of water undertakers.

Annex B

Domestic water supply duty

7 The Water Industry Act 1991 goes on to distinguish between the domestic supply duty and supplies for non-domestic purposes. The meaning of "domestic purposes" in relation to water supply is defined in section 218 of that Act as water used for drinking, washing, cooking, central heating or sanitary purposes. Where the whole or any part of premises are for occupation as a house, domestic purposes includes water used for the purposes of a profession carried on it that house.

8 Domestic purposes also includes those outside the house (including the washing of vehicles and the watering of gardens) which are connected with the occupation of the house and which may be satisfied by water drawn from a tap inside the house and without the use of a hosepipe or similar apparatus. Use of water in a bath having a capacity of more than 230 litres (that is, about three times the occupied capacity of a typical domestic bath) is also excluded from "domestic purposes", as is that used for the purposes of the business of laundries or for preparing food or drink for consumption off the premises.

9 The domestic supply duty in relation to any premises is a duty, under section 52 of that Act, to provide a supply of water sufficient for domestic purposes and to maintain the connection between the water company's main and the premises' service pipe. This duty extends to all new premises and water undertakers are therefore required to supply water to meet new domestic demands, irrespective of their water resource position.

10 Under section 54 of the Act, the domestic supply duty is owed to the consumer. Unless resulting from extreme measures taken under a Drought Order, any breach of that duty which causes loss or damage to be sustained by a consumer provides grounds for civil action by the consumer against the water undertaker, although a company able to show that it took all reasonable steps and exercised all due diligence to avoid the breach has that defence. There are no other powers of enforcement specifically in respect of the domestic supply duty, although the enforcement provision in respect of the general duty under section 37 clearly embraces domestic supplies.

Constancy and pressure of domestic water supplies

11 The duty to maintain supplies is given further expression in section 65 of the Water Industry Act 1991 which requires water undertakers to 'cause the water in such of its water mains and other pipes which are used for providing supplies of water for domestic purposes.... to be laid on constantly and at such a pressure as will cause the water to reach to the top-most storey of every building within the undertaker's area'. The pressure requirement does not extend to the supply to a height greater than that which would be reached by gravity flow from a nominated service reservoir or tank.

12 The duty in respect of constancy and pressure is enforceable under section 18 of the Act by the Secretary of State. In addition, under section 65(10), breach of the duty constitutes an offence rendering the undertaker liable to a fine, unless the undertaker shows that it took all reasonable steps and exercised all due diligence to avoid the commission of the offence.

Other supplies

13 Where supplies are requested for other than domestic purposes, it is the duty of the water undertaker under section 55(2) of the Act to provide that supply. A water undertaker is under no obligation to provided a new supply to any premises for non-domestic purposes if its provision would put at risk the water undertaker's ability to meet its existing obligations in respect of water supply for all purposes or its ability to meet likely future demands for domestic supplies.

Quality of water supplies

14 Under section 68 of the Water Industry Act 1991, water undertakers, when supplying water to any premises for domestic or food production purposes, have the duty to supply only water which is wholesome at the time of supply. Water is regarded as wholesome if the requirements set out in regulation 3 of the Water Supply (Water Quality) Regulations 1989 (as amended in 1989 and 1991) are met.

15 The activities of water undertakers in respect of water supply are at all time subject to the requirement for the supplies to be wholesome. This is a requirement enforceable by the Secretary of State under section 18 of the Water Industry Act 1991. The Secretary of State may also prosecute water undertakers for the offence of supplying water unfit for human consumption under section 70 of the Act – water unfit will be unwholesome but the reverse is not necessarily true. Technical assessment of drinking water quality and advice to the Secretary of State on enforcement action or on prosecution is provided by the Drinking Water Inspectorate.

Information on water supplies

16   Under section 188 of the Water Resources Act 1991, the Environment Agency now has the duty to collate and publish information from which assessments can be made of the actual and prospective demand for water in England and Wales.

17   The Director has the duty, under section 27(2) of the Water Industry Act 1991, so far as is practicable to collect information relating to any matters for which he has duties or powers. Such matters of course include the provision of water supplies. The Secretary of State may give directions in this respect under section 27(3) of that Act, although none has been made to date. The Director is required by section 193 of that Act to make an annual report to the Secretary of State giving a general survey of matters falling within the scope of the Director's functions and is empowered to prepare whatever other reports appear to him to be expedient in that respect.

18   Section 201 of the Water Industry Act 1991 empowers the Secretary of State and the Director to publish information on any water undertaker's conduct of its duties. Water undertakers have the duty, under section 202 of that Act, to provide the Secretary of State with whatever information he may reasonably require in respect of the carrying out of its functions. Enforceable powers of direction are available under section 202(4). Furthermore, where it appears to the Secretary of State or the Director that a water undertaker may be contravening, or has contravened any statutory requirement, either may serve notice requiring the provision of relevant information. Failure to comply would constitute an offence under section 203(4).

19   Under the Water Supply (Water Quality) Regulations 1989 (as amended in 1989 and 1991), water undertakers are required to maintain a public record containing details of the quality of its drinking water supplies and to provide free access to this record by the public during reasonable hours. Water undertakers also are required to publish annual reports on drinking water quality. These requirements are enforceable by

the Secretary of State under section 18 of the Water Industry Act 1991.

Duty to promote the efficient use of water by customers

20   Schedule 22 of the Environment Act 1995 has inserted into the Water Industry Act 1991 section 93A which gives every water undertaker the duty to promote the efficient use of water by its customers, enforceable by the Secretary of State or the Director. The Director has the power to require water undertakers to take specific action or to achieve specific overall standards of performance in respect of this duty.

Prevention of contamination or waste of water

21   Anyone guilty of any act or neglect which causes water for public supply in a water undertaker's works, mains or other pipes to be contaminated commits an offence under section 72 of the Water Industry Act 1991 and is liable to penalties including imprisonment.

22   If the owner or occupier of any premises intentionally or negligently causes contamination, wastage or undue consumption of water by or through fittings for which he is responsible, he commits an offence under section 73 of the Water Industry Act 1991 and is liable to a fine. Section 75 of the Act empowers a water undertaker to serve notice on a consumer requiring him to take corrective action or, in emergency, to cut off the supply. Section 74 of the Act empowers the Secretary of State to make regulations for preventing contamination or waste from water fittings.

Charging for water

23   Water undertakers are empowered by section 142 of the Water Industry Act 1991 to 'fix charges for any services provided in the course of carrying out its functions' and may 'fix charges… by reference to such matters, and may adopt such methods and principles for the calculation and imposition of the charges, as appear to the undertaker to be appropriate'.

24   The Director is required, by section 2(3) of the Water Industry Act 1991, to exercise and perform his duties in the manner that he considers best calculated to protect the interests of customers as respects the fixing and recovery of water charges, and in particular to see that no undue preference or discrimination is shown in fixing charges.

Annex B

Hosepipe bans

25 If a water undertaker is of the opinion that a serious shortage of water for supply exists or is threatened (for whatever reason), it can, under section 76 of the Water Industry Act 1991, restrict or prohibit the use of hosepipes or similar apparatus for garden water or washing private vehicles. Anyone breaching a hosepipe ban is guilty of an offence. There is no statutory entitlement to compensation for losses resulting from hosepipe bans, other than in respect of a partial reduction in the charges for the use of a hosepipe which some companies may make.

Water use restrictions under drought orders

26 A water undertaker can apply to the Secretary of State for the imposition, using his powers under section 70 of the Water Resources Act 1991, of a drought order in any part of its area. Under an ordinary drought order, the water undertaker may be authorised to restrict the use of water for a range of non-essential purposes currently specified in the Drought Direction 1991. Other obligations upon the water undertaker as regards water supply may also be suspended or modified. An emergency drought order may additionally enable the water undertaker to restrict the use of water for any purpose and to supply water by means of standpipes or water tanks.

27 In making any drought order, the Secretary of State has to be satisfied that a serious deficiency in the water supply exists or is threatened because of an exceptional shortage of rain. In making an emergency drought order, he also has to be satisfied that the water shortage is likely to impair the economic or social well-being of people in the area. Applications for drought orders have to be advertised by the water undertaker and objections have to considered by the Secretary of State in reaching a decision on the application. Anyone breaching restrictions on water use imposed under a drought order is guilty of an offence. There is presently no statutory entitlement for water consumers to compensation for loss of water supply under the provisions of a drought order.

Water resource management

28 Under section 6(2) of the Environment Act 1995, the Environment Agency has the duty 'to take all such action as it may from time to time consider, in accordance with any directions [given by Ministers under section 40 of the Act] to be necessary or expedient for the purpose -

(a) of conserving, redistributing or otherwise augmenting water resources in England and Wales; and

(b) of securing the proper use of water resources in England and Wales.'

29 To the extent that it considers appropriate for carrying out these duties, the Environment Agency has, under section 20(1) of the Water Resources Act 1991, a duty, so far as is reasonably practicable, to enter into and maintain arrangements with water undertakers for securing the proper management or operation of water resources available for their use and of any reservoirs, apparatus or other works under their control.

30 Although section 20(2)(c) of that Act requires questions arising under such arrangements once made to be referred for determination to the Secretary of State or the Director, there are currently no powers under which the Environment Agency can compel water undertakers to enter into new arrangements. Obligations upon water undertakers under such arrangements are enforceable by the Secretary of State under section 18 of the Water Industry Act 1991.

31 Section 40 of the Water Industry Act 1991 as substituted by section 44 of the Competition and Service (Utilities) Act 1992 enables the Director, on application of a water undertaker, to make an order requiring another water undertaker to give a bulk supply of raw or treated water to the applicant on whatever terms and conditions are specified in the order. In making the order, it has to appear to the Director that the application is necessary or expedient for the purposes of securing the efficient use of water resources or the efficient supply of water, and the Director has to consult the Environment Agency. The Director also has to consider the effect of the application on the supplying water undertaker's ability to meet its existing and likely future obligations to supply water. There is no provision by which a water undertaker can be compelled to apply for a bulk supply.

Abstraction licensing

32 Under section 24 of the Water Resources Act 1991, abstraction licences are required for all significant abstractions from ground or surface water resources. Licences are administered by the Environment Agency. Under section 37 of that Act, applications for new licences have to be advertised and notice of application has to be served on the relevant water undertaker if not from that body. Representations made as a result of that process have to be taken into account by the Agency in determining the application. If the application is turned down, the applicant may appeal to the Secretary of State. Section 41 of the Act empowers the Secretary of State to direct that applications for licences be determined by him rather than the Agency and his decision is final, subject to application to the High Court.

33 Under section 35 of the Water Resources Act 1991, applications for abstraction licences can only be made by the occupier of the land from which the abstraction is to take place. Section 49 of the Act provides for the succession of licences when there is change in the occupation of the whole of the land specified in the licence as the land on which the abstracted water is to be used; provided the new occupier gives notice to the Environment Agency within 15 months of the change in occupation the licence passes to that new occupier. Section 50 of the Act provides for succession where there is a change in occupation of only part of the relevant land.

34 Provision exists, under section 52 of the Act, for the modification or revocation of licences by the Environment Agency or the Secretary of State. Unless the existing licence holder has voluntarily sought revocation, has failed to comply with licence conditions or has failed to abstract any water for at least seven years, compensation is payable to him for any deleterious effect of modification or revocation.

Drought orders and permits

35 A water undertaker can make application to the Secretary of State for the imposition, using his powers under section 70 of the Water Resources Act 1991, of an ordinary or emergency drought order in any part of its area (see paragraph 26f). Under either type of drought order, the water undertaker may be authorised to take more than the licensed amount of water from existing sources or to use new sources. It may also be authorised to reduce compensation water flows from reservoirs to watercourses. Where such measures are not also associated with application for water use restrictions, a water undertaker may now apply to the Environment Agency for a drought permit under section 79A of the Water Resources Act 1991 as inserted by paragraph 140 of schedule 22 to the Environment Act 1995. Applications, whether for Orders or Permits, have to be processed by the relevant authority as outlined in paragraph 27 above.

Information on water resources

36 Under section 188 of the Water Resources Act 1991, the Environment Agency has the duty to collate and publish information from which assessments can be made of the actual and prospective water resources available in England and Wales.

37 The Environment Agency may give directions, under section 201 of the Water Resources Act 1991, requiring a water abstractor to provide information 'as to the abstraction' in whatever form and at whatever time the Agency may specify. The abstractor may make representations to the Secretary of State if the direction is considered unreasonable or unduly onerous. Failure to comply with directions constitutes an offence with a liability to a fine.

General environmental duties relevant to water resources and supplies

38 The Secretary of State, the Director and every company holding appointment as a water undertaker each have a duty, under section 3(2) of the Water Industry Act 1991 to exercise their powers so as: (i) to further the conservation and enhancement of natural beauty and the conservation of flora, fauna and geographical or physiographical features of special interest; (ii) to have regard to the desirability of protecting and conserving buildings, sifters and objectors of archaeological, architectural or historic interest; and (iii) to take into account any effects which their proposals would have on the beauty or amenity of any rural or urban area or on any such flora, fauna, features, buildings, sites or objects. Obligations of water undertaker which result from these provisions are enforceable by the Secretary of State under section 18 of the Act, as also are any obligations in respect of sites of special interests arising from application of section 4 of the Act.

39 Ministers and the Environment Agency have, under sections 7 and 8 of the Environment Act 1995, similar wide ranging duties in respect of formulating or considering proposals relevant to the functions of water undertakers. The Environment Agency has, under section 6(1) of that Act, the duty to promote the conservation and enhancement of the natural beauty and amenity of inland waters and of land associated with such waters, the conservation of flora and fauna which are dependent on an aquatic environment, and the use of such waters and land for recreational purposes.

Annex C.

INFLUENCING WATER DEMAND: SOME EXPERIENCES FROM OTHER COUNTRIES

Introduction

1   This annex has been drawn up by the Department of the Environment and examines available information on various factors which have been used to influence demand for water in parts of some other countries. Whilst it is important to bear in mind that a variety of other factors have a bearing on water consumption in different countries, this information nevertheless provides some illustration of the scope and effects of demand management by the means described.

2   Some evidence on the factors influencing the demand for water is available from 1980s work (OECD, 1987b). The key points are briefly re-iterated here and tables of elasticities are reproduced in Table 2 at the end of this annex.

Price elasticities and tariffs

3   The first need is to consider the evidence of the effects of price on consumption and how that might be influenced by the type of tariff implemented. The OECD work summarises empirical estimates in a number of industrial countries for price elasticities in its 1987 study (OECD, 1987b). It notes that, in all but one case, year-round domestic price elasticities significantly different from zero have been found, and suggests an average range of -0.3/-0.05 (see Table 2). It appears that no new studies have radically changed this conclusion.

4   Whilst these average price elasticities are low, the more interesting aspects from the UK point of view are the elasticities of demand for in-house versus ex-house use and peak as opposed to average elasticities. Also of interest is evidence of the potential one-off savings resulting from introducing a price incentive attendant on switching from flat-rate charging to metered, volumetric charging.

5   The low elasticities noted above for average use have been requoted as relevant for in-house demand (Boland, 1996). American research confirms that ex-house use is more price elastic (-0.5/-1.5, depending *inter alia* on climate) than in-house. The most comprehensive US study (Danielson 1979) found an elasticity for sprinkler demand of -1.38 and for in-house use of -0.3 in an area utilizing block pricing. The conclusions were that pricing policies should take account of the different elasticities for in- and ex-house use, and if appropriately designed, could have a large

influence on ex-house demands. Another study from the USA (Williams and Suh, 1986) showed that marginal pricing had little effect on demand in commercial property where the owner, not the individual user, was responsible for payment. All the time-series studies concluded that the weather (average temperature, daylight hours, average rainfall) was a strong explanatory variable for demand.

6   The effect of price on peak demands has to be derived at present from such evidence as this on sprinkler demand and other evidence on the response of demand to seasonal tariffs. Herrington (Herrington, 1996), referring to a recent Ernst and Young survey of tariff details for 121 US utilities, notes that seasonal tariffs are few and far between (only applying in 12 of these cases). He reports that studies in the 1980s recorded reductions of between 10% and 15% in system peak day ratios following the introduction of seasonal tariffs in four utilities. The most recent survey of the USA (Raftelis, 1993) reveals that declining block tariffs have dwindled in use from 60% to 46% of the major utilities between 1986 and 1992. Conservation rate structures (defined as uniform or rising block) replaced these structures and are now used in 54% of utilities. The transitional effects of the new rate structures in four utilities operating in the North East of the USA are discussed in more detail below.

7   Tariff structure offers important possibilities in terms of maximising incentives to demand restraint. This might be through differential tariff rates for different uses (for example, in-house versus ex-house) and also through tariff structures such as increasing block tariffs, two-part tariffs *etc.*. These all have different strengths and weaknesses to achieve efficiency and equity criteria. For example, despite reservations about their efficiency, increasing block tariffs (generally justified on social equity grounds) have been found to have significant effects in terms of reducing demand in a number of countries, for example Switzerland, Italy, Denmark and Japan (Herrington, 1996). The range of experience from other countries in implementing new tariff structures is discussed in the following paragraphs.

Examples of tariffs and their effects

8   In 1968, the utility company in Zurich, **Switzerland** replaced a steeply declining block tariff system with an increasing block tariff. Tariffs were redesigned with an aim of reducing the rapid rate of growth in water consumption, which had seen a two-fold rise in a 25 year period up to 1970. The two-part progressive structure introduced the idea of 'excess consumption':

for a consumer with a particular meter size in 1975, this was defined as double the 1974 average consumption for consumers with that particular meter size. Price in the 'excess' block was twice that in the 'basic block' and it was the size of the lower block that varied between consumer groups, not the price. 'Excess' consumption has since been curbed and consumption by 'normal' users stabilized.

9 **Italy** began to reform its tariff structure in the mid 1970s. By 1979, water boards set tariffs to yield revenue that covered average consumptive costs, allocating an initial allowance with low prices for the first 200-267 litres/property/day and thereafter charging on an increasing block schedule. Rome recorded a 1.8% reduction in domestic consumption between 1974-78, with Turin and Naples seeing a 5.2% and 2.8% fall respectively in *per capita* consumption over the same period. Economic recession has explained some of the fall, but most is attributed to the effects of the new tariffs.

10 Both these types of tariff structure appear to have had an impact on consumption. Rising block tariffs can provide a strong incentive to conserve water but, because of equity concerns, a 'lifeline' allowance to meet essential uses is often set aside, allocating a designated quantity of water at low or zero rates. Examples of the use of such 'lifeline' allowances have been reported in Japan, Greece, Belgium and Portugal (OECD, 1987b).

11 Such equity considerations were largely ignored in **Australia** by the Perth Metropolitan Water Board in 1978. Resource sustainability was being threatened by rising domestic consumption, large scale capital expenditure was required and yet consumers expected ever higher levels of environmental protection and standards of service. To make consumers meet the full costs of providing the service and also to curb demands, the Water Board introduced a two-part 'pay for service/pay for use' tariff structure. Rather than extend a generous 'lifeline' allowance to all households, the initial 'pay for service' allowance was kept deliberately small so that over 90% of households were confronted with a 'pay for use' volumetric charge. The volumetric charge rose by 22% in real terms between 1979 and 1983 and average consumption fell by 20-30% over the period.

12 Another two-part tariff scheme in **Australia** was introduced to the residential sector in the Hunter District in 1982-83. A flat-rate structure was replaced by a simple two-part tariff, considered 'the closest practicable approach to efficient pricing'. The fixed part of the tariff aimed at covering the fixed costs of the availability of the service (about 55% of the Board's costs) with the variable component to producing revenue to cover the remaining variable operating costs. In 1982, on the introduction of the new tariff structure and complete metering, average consumption had fallen by 31%, peak day consumption by 50% and distribution losses by 33%.

13 Conservation tariffs and programmes have recently been implemented by four utilities on the North Eastern seaboard of the **USA**, with varying degrees of success. Reductions in total demand ranged between 6% and 23%, with several different tariff formulas used. The exact effect of each tariff structure is hard to determine as they are often used alongside other conservation measures that enable consumers to reduce their consumption, such as more water efficient appliances, and are not adjusted for other socio-economic factors that may be influencing demand. United Water in New York uses a summer peak rate 50% higher than the winter rate that has produced a fall in total demand by 6% since 1993, and reducing the winter:summer peak ratio from 1.8 to 1.5. New York City Water Board enforced universal metering using a uniform tariff structure and experienced a steady fall in consumption of 11% between 1990 and 1995, even with the advent of some of the hottest summers on record. The Boston area uses either standard volumetric charging or rising-block and has had a more dramatic 23% fall in demand. It has enforced new plumbing codes and vigorously monitored and repaired leakages (targeted at 5% of the public water supply). The result has been an indefinite delay in new resource development. United Water has also achieved a postponement of resource development but for only 5-6 years.

14 The examples from the USA show the potential of tariffs to abate demands. However, the authors of these programmes recognized that while metering and conservation tariff design are critical to their effectiveness, only the installation of water efficient technology alongside the tariffs will ensure **permanent** savings. Incentives through prices, regulation or education all inform the consumer of the need to conserve, for example choosing water efficient equipment when existing equipment is being replaced. To realise the full extent of savings, New York City Water Board itself decided to 'empower' the consumer with the means to reduce demand, finding it economic to offer rebates to households for replacing high volume flush toilets and showerheads. The authors of the scheme argued that, without this assistance, the customer would feel that

Annex C.

compulsory metering simply increased water bills without being given the chance to achieve savings; the scheme would have produced resentment and the full extent of conservation would not have been attained. In contrast to this determined conservation programme, commentators felt that the water authorities in Cape May, New Jersey had not realized the full potential savings of its metering policy by failing to back it up with replacement of inefficient, water hungry hardware. Some 'bounce-back' in demand was subsequently recorded in the area, although at a slower growth rate than before the introduction of the programme.

Metering

15   The results from the UK's metering trials are well known but an extensive search has found little foreign evidence to supplement this. One commentator (Boland, 1996) remarks that where metering is being introduced today (for example, in Buenos Aires, **Argentina**), there is a general failure to record the effects. The main source remains the 1980s work (OECD, 1987a) which listed 22 studies with reported demand reductions of 10-30%.

16   One example referred to in the OECD publication is Moss, **Norway** where in 1978 some 5,000 meters covering 100% of the population of 25,000 were installed. On their introduction, prices were raised and a waste water tariff was added. Between 1978 and 1984, daily total demand fell by 28% from 16,575 m³/day to 11,950 m³/day. Peak day demand also fell from about 23,000 m³/day in 1978 to about 16,000 m³/day in 1979 (a fall of 30%) and recorded a low figure of 13,000 m³/day in 1983. Another publication (Coopers and Lybrand, 1985) presents evidence from Hjorring, Denmark which in the early 1970s had a 10% decline in total consumption; Brest, France, where there was a 27% reduction in domestic per capita consumption in the mid-1960s; and from Utrecht, Netherlands where in the late 1970s metering was found to have decreased consumption by 10% after 12 to 18 months had elapsed since its introduction.

17   A study in Boulder, Colorado, USA looked at domestic consumption patterns after a two year metering programme had been completed in 1963. The ratio of actual sprinkler use to potential sprinkler use requirements over the period fell by between 39% and 64% of the previous value. In-house use was also 36% lower than the estimated figure before 1961. In a follow-up study by Hanke in the same town two years later, residents demonstrated no signs of complacency in water

use, with most intensifying their attitude to water conservation. This was particularly marked with outside uses, especially sprinklers.

18   Denmark has different metering practices for town and rural homes. Town houses are generally metered whereas rural areas face a flat rate. Herrington (Herrington, 1996) finds that consumption in councils covering 40% of the population had fallen from a steady 170-175 litres/head/day (l/h/d) over 1983-89 to 158 l/h/d in 1992. He attributes this fall to the increases in the volumetric charges for water (20%) and sewerage (22%) between 1983 and 1992, a rise of 65% in real terms.

19   The Netherlands has seen an increase in consumption from 107 l/h/d to 135 l/h/d over the period 1980-1992. Meter coverage in the country is high but the picture is distorted by the practice in large towns where, for historical reasons, properties have never been metered. Around one third of the country's dwellings are flats. Over the whole country, 24% of the properties – mainly in the large conurbations – are charged a flat rate, whilst the rest of the country is metered. Achttienribbe, in a report for the Netherlands Waterworks Association (VEWIN, 1992) examining the micro-components of demand, attributes the rise in consumption between 1980-92 to increased consumption from showering. Showers have a 99% market penetration, and the report noted that the frequency of use and the volume used per shower had increased substantially over the period. Consumption from showering was also found to vary widely between large towns (51 l/h/d), where flat rates are used, against a national average of 39 l/h/d. The extent to which this urban differential can be explained by factors other than the rate structure was not explored.

20   The VEWIN report discussed various possible tariff schemes that could be implemented. It suggests that tariffs would have to be raised by twice their current levels for them to have an impact on demand. However, raising tariffs and introducing metering would not necessarily be under the duress of resource shortages but from the need to be seen to be acting responsibly. There was a strong sense that they did not want to appear profligate with their use of water: if this is correct, then the pattern of stabilization seen in Germany could reoccur in the Netherlands. Herrington (OECD, 1987b), for example, found that one water authority in the Netherlands intended to meter domestic customers on the basis that metering will result in greater equity between customers: its expectation was that domestic consumption would decline by only 6% and reducing consumption was not the primary objective of the policy.

21   These types of result mirror the findings of the metering trials on the Isle of Wight and several small scale sites. There is very little evidence – and none of that is conclusive – of demand grow-back after the introduction of metering.

Domestic per capita consumption

22   Sample domestic per capita consumption data in other northern European countries is available (Herrington, 1996) for comparison to UK data and is summarised in Table 1. No further data were uncovered in the course of preparing this annex.

23   The figures in Table 2 show the behaviour in domestic per capita consumption in Northern European countries since 1970. Factors that have influenced domestic demand vary between countries, and each has its own 'water culture' that should be considered when explaining the trend in demand. Some explanation of the behaviour in the Netherlands and Denmark has been given in the preceding paragraphs.

24   Germany is unusual in achieving a stable per capita consumption for the past ten years. This is possibly due to increased meter penetration and the zealous greening of German society raising awareness of the full cost of water, although the exact extent that any measure has had on demand is hard to establish. Metering, for instance, is unlikely to explain entirely the stabilisation since only 30-40% of the population are directly metered. The remainder live in apartment blocks where separate dwellings are not individually metered (though hot water often is), so the individual may not face the full cost of consumption. More evidence will be needed before drawing firm conclusions as to why the stabilisation has occurred and as to the relevance of the German experience to other countries.

25   The example of Germany demonstrates that factors peculiar to that country alone may be responsible for the stabilization, and this must be taken into account before drawing parallels to any other country. Direct comparisons are further confounded by different data collection methods and different definitions of component use. Efforts by the European Environment Agency and Eurostat are under way to try to find a uniform methodology. Inter-country comparisons may be useful in informing the debate and the extent that various demand management options can take effect; however, transposition of that experience into this country should be done with due caution, taking into account the full range of circumstances that produced the result.

Annex C.

References

Boland, 1996. Personal communication with Prof J Boland, John Hopkins University, Baltimore, USA.

Coopers and Lybrand Associates, 1985. *Water Metering*. Department of the Environment, 1985.

Danielson, L.E., 1979. *Analysis of residential demand for water using micro time-series data*. Water Resources Research, 1979.

Herrington, P., *Pricing Water Properly*. University of Leicester Discussion Paper, 1996.

OECD, 1987a. *Water demand forecasting in OECD countries*. Organisation for Economic Co-operation and Development, Paris, 1987.

OECD, 1987b. *Pricing of Water Services*. Organisation for Economic Co-operation and Development, Paris, 1987.

Raftelis, G.A., 1993. *Comprehensive Guide to Water and Wastewater Finance and Pricing*. Lewis Publishing, 1993.

VEWIN, 1992. *Water Savings in the Netherlands. Final Report*. Netherlands, 1994.

Williams, M., and Suh, B., 1986. *The demand for urban water by customer class*. Applied Economics, 1986.

Table 1: Recent domestic *per capita* consumption trends in Europe (l/h/d).

	1970	1975	1980	1985	1988/89	1991
Austria	121	130	130	131	145	
Belgium	72	93	103	108	108	116
Denmark		174	175	191	190	175
Germany*	118	133	140	145	145	144
Finland			148	155	151	150
France		106	109	141	159	161
Netherlands	119	133	141	157	167	173
Sweden	229	207	196	195	194	195
Switzerland*	270	258	229	259	270	260

* includes small business use

Table 2: Price elasticities for urban public water supply (from OEDC 1987a)

Country	Location	Type of Study	Estimated price elasticity	Reference
Australia	971 households in 20 groups in Perth	readings 1976-82: pooled x-section and time series	Overall -0.11	Metropolitan Water Authority 1985
Australia	315 households in Perth	x-section (hypothetical valuation technique)	in-house: -0.04 ex-house: -0.31 overall: -0.18	Thomas, Syme and Gosselink 1983
Australia	137 households in Toowoomba, Queensland	1972-3 to 1976-7 pooled x-section and time series	short-term: -0.26 long-term: -0.75	Gallagher et al 1981
Canada	Urban demand in eastern Canada	x-section in 1960s	winter: -0.75 summer: -1.07	Grima 1972
Canada	Municipal demand Victoria, B.C.	time series 1954-70	winter: -0.58 summer: zero mid-peak: -0.25 year-round: 0.40	Sewell and Roueche 1974
Finland	Municipal demand, Helsinki	time series	year-round: 0.11	Laukkanen 1981
Netherlands	Industrial demand, Rotterdam	time series, 1960s and 1970s	no price elasticity found	Rotterdam Water Authority 1976
Sweden	69 domestic residences, Malmo	14 readings each over 1971-78: pooled x-section and time series	year-round: - 0.15	Hanke and De Mare 1982
USA	2159 households in Tucson, Arizona	42 readings each over 42 months 1976-79. Pooled x-section and time series	year-round: - 0.256	Martin, Ingram, Laney and Griffin 1983
USA	Domestic use in Tucson, Arizona	time series 1974-77	year-round: log model: -0.27 linear: -0.45/-0.61	Billings and Agthe 1980
USA	Residential use in 21 study areas, eastern and western USA	x-section early 1960s	winter: -0.06 summer: - 0.57 (east) - 0.43 (west)	Howe 1982

Annex D

contributed by the Environment Agency

STANDARDS OF BEST PRACTICE FOR GROUNDWATER YIELD ASSESSMENT

Introduction

1. The purpose of this annex, contributed by the Environment Agency, is to outline the principles for the assessment of yields of groundwater sources. The principles described are based on the results of a project commissioned by the water industry and completed in March 1995 (Beeson et al., 1995). **The approach set out in this annex is open to further consultation and development with the water industry and independent expert organisations, particularly in the light of the material presented in the main report.** Comments should be sent by 6 December 1996 to: The Director of Water Management, The Environment Agency, Rio House, Waterside Drive, Aztec West, Almondsbury, Bristol, BS12 4UD.

2. In summary, the suggested approach is to determine for each source or group of sources:

◆ the average recorded deployed output of the source during a period when groundwater levels were at a minimum during the worst drought on record and which did not cause unacceptable environmental impact – an important estimate of yield for resource planning purposes;

◆ the average recorded peak week deployed output of the source during the period of the worst historic drought, which did not cause unacceptable environmental impact, but not necessarily when groundwater levels were actually at an all-time low – this estimate of yield is particularly relevant to the ability of the source to meet short term demand and the design of the distribution system; and

◆ the average or peak week potential yield which is the maximum possible deployable output of the source under thesame drought conditions as above, constrained only by the well or aquifer properties – this is the yield which could be obtained assuming specified changes to the source works and any consequent variations to the abstraction licence.

Yield definitions

3. The water industry and regulators have been developing a glossary of definitions for use in water resources planning and operations. These are summarised in Figure 1. Key definitions based on this figure for groundwater yield are as follows:

◆ **Deployable Output** – the output of a commissioned source or group of sources as constrained by:

    – licence, if applicable;
    – water quality;
    – environment;
    – treatment;
    – raw water mains and/or aqueducts;
    – pumping plant and/or well/aquifer properties;
    – transfer and/or output main for specified conditions and demands.

◆ **Potential Yield** – the yield of a commissioned source or group of sources as constrained only by well and/or aquifer properties for specified conditions and demands.

◆ **Hydrological Yield** – the natural output of a source (as constructed) that can be supported by the catchment or aquifer feeding the sources and which is equivalent to the average recharge for a critical drought duration. This particular definition of yield is included here for completeness only.

◆ **Outage** – a temporary loss of Deployable Output due to planned or unplanned events. Planned events are those such as maintenance of sourceworks; unplanned events are exclusively pollution, turbidity, nitrate, algae, power failure and system failure.

◆ **Water Available for Use** – the Deployable Output of a source less deductions made for allowable outage and planning allowances. This will be the yield figure used for detailed resource planning purposes.

Type of Analysis

4. The methodology for the assessment of the yield of groundwater sources requires consideration of:

◆ the ability of the source to meet short-term (average day peak week demand – ADPW) and average demands under drought conditions; and

◆ the operationalconstraints on output, including pump capacity and intake level, abstraction licence conditions, treatment works capacity.

Water level and demand conditions

5. The yield of a groundwater source is determined by a complex interplay between the aquifer charac-

teristics, particularly storage and transmissivity and a number of factors including:

- the water level in the well during a severe drought;
- the peak and average rates of pumping; and
- the well construction and associated hydraulics which determine the potential yield of the source.

Drought

6. The antecedent water level for the source is defined by the year when groundwater levels fell to their all-time minimum values in the area of the source, as indicated by long term records, preferably on a monthly basis, from one or more local observation wells. Although a few records with more than 100 years of data exist, more records date from the early 1960s or 1970s giving between 35 and 25 years of record. However, at least two severe groundwater droughts have occurred within the last 25 years, so many records show significant drought minima.

7. The drought of 1988 – 1992 was remarkably protracted causing groundwater levels to reach an all-time low in some areas of the UK, notably in the east and south west England. In other areas, the 1976 drought had a greater impact on levels. The concept of return period or frequency of occurrence is not therefore a part of the proposed methodology.

Peak and average rates of pumping

8. Peak output and average output place particular demands on groundwater sources during periods of drought and need to be taken into consideration in resource planning studies.

9. The methodology for the assessment of the deployable output of groundwater sources for the condition of peak week demand requires inspection of the distribution input record to determine the ADPW for the worst drought to have affected the area of the particular source. The high pumping rates during such periods are critical short term conditions for groundwater sources and can cause water levels to drop to levels which can be difficult to sustain. The sustainable rate of peak output identified from the pumping records under these critical conditions is an important factor for meeting short term peaks in demand, typically during hot, dry weather.

10. In the case of average demand, critical output assessments are based on monthly distribution input data for those months when groundwater levels were at a minimum during the worst drought on record. For those aquifers which recess rapidly, it is more appropriate to determine the output from weekly rather than monthly data.

11. These historic values of average and peak deployable output under drought conditions are based on operational experience and should be further constrained if necessary to ensure that the quoted figures of 'deployable output' make due allowance for all current constraints including:

- licensed quantities;
- environmental constraints such as effects on wetlands and river flows;
- quality constraints; and
- sourceworks constraints (which may have been imposed since the drought year used for the study).

Well construction

12. The average and peak week deployable outputs described above are based on the historic operational performance of the groundwater source and do not necessarily represent the potential yield of the well or borehole. The potential yield of a source is the yield corresponding to the deepest advisable pumping water level (DAPWL) below which undesirable effects begin to occur.

13. In some cases the DAPWL will be controlled by features of the well construction, such as the base of the solid casing on the top of an adit, or by features of the aquifer system, such as the base of the confining layer. If these are not a constraint, the DAPWL should be set to a depth so as to prevent a significant reduction in output were the level to reduce further.

Other considerations

14. Further consideration can be given to defining deployable output and potential yield using an analytical rather than operational approach where, for example, the source has not been fully utilised. An analytical approach requires measurements of drawdown for a range of outputs for continuous pumping lasting 200 days (average demand) or seven days (peak demand). Analytical methods can then be used to define the average and peak demands for the particular source using the pumping test data.

Annex D

contributed by the Environment Agency

Auditability

15.   A key factor of any methodology will be the requirement to demonstrate the assumptions and constraints used in the yield assessment calculations. The audit trail must be capable of inspection and verification by independent certifiers and the regulators. The suggested methodology has a tabular and graphical form of assessment which provides the basis for a suitable form of audit. Attention will focus in the audit on the constraints on the deployable output, particularly where this is significantly below the potential yield of the source or the licensed quantity.

Reference

Beeson, S., van Wonderen, J., and Misstear, B, 1995. *A Methodology for the Determination of Outputs of Groundwater Sources*, UK Water Industry Research Limited, London, 1995.

Annex D

contributed by the Environment Agency

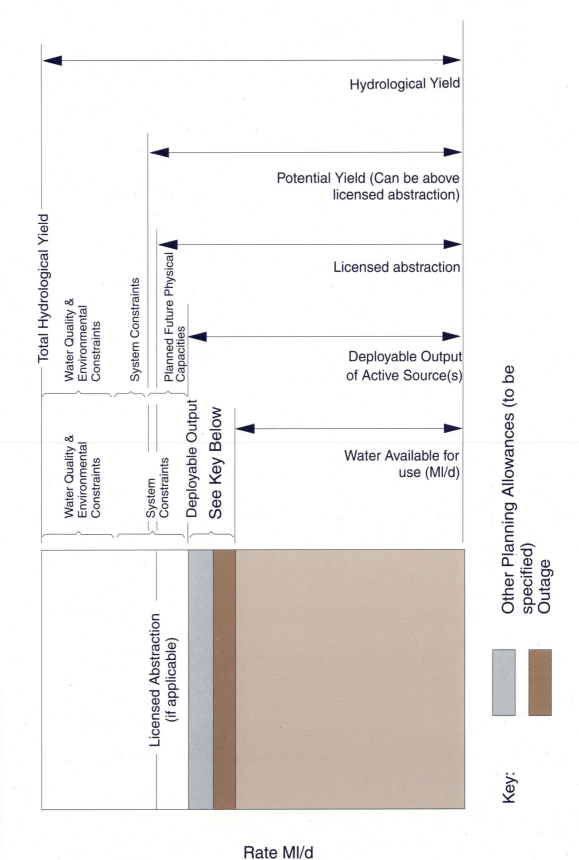

Figure 1. Terms used in the definitions of the output of an active source or group of active sources

Annex E

contributed by the Environment Agency

STANDARDS OF BEST PRACTICE FOR SURFACE WATER YIELD ASSESSMENT

Introduction

1.   The purpose of this annex, contributed by the Environment Agency, is to outline the principles for the framework for the assessment of surface water. Whilst this framework is not yet fully developed, it can still be regarded as a significant step towards best practice and is based on the results of a recent project commissioned by the National Rivers Authority. **The approach set out in this annex is open to further consultation and development with the water industry and independent expert organisations, particularly in the light of the material presented in the main report.** Comments should be sent by **6 December 1996** to: The Director of Water Management, The Environment Agency, Rio House, Waterside Drive, Aztec West, Almondsbury, Bristol, BS12 4UD.

Type of analysis

2.   The methodology for surface water yield assessment should:

◆   simulate the realistic operation of the water resources systems in question; and

◆   calculate the yield as the supply which can be met with a given Level of Service.

Simulation

3.   The yield of the system in question should be simulated over as long a period as possible. Some water resources systems could fail to meet demand during dry periods occurring before the start of the specific hydrological record. These so called critical periods may occur as far back as the late 19th century in some cases, and consideration should therefore be given to generating flow records back to the appropriate period.

Yield definitions

4.   The definitions for surface water yield are in line with those which the industry have been developing for water resources planning and operational purposes. These are summarised in Figure 1 and described below:

Deployable Output – the term to be used to describe the useable yield of a system. Deployable Output is the constant rate of supply that can be maintained from the water resources system except during periods of restriction within the following constraints[1]:

◆   given level of service;

◆   the historic period for which data is available;

◆   supply without storage entering the emergency storage zone (see paragraph 12);

◆   supply within the defined physical capacities (of the existing system) adopted for the simulation;

◆   source operation in accordance with the licence or by, prior agreement with the Environment Agency, a Drought Order or Permit; and

◆   water quality and environmentalconsiderations.

Potential Yield – if some future physical capacities are included in the simulation then the resulting yield would be the Potential Yield with those assumed capacities.

Hydrological Yield – the traditional Hydrological Yield is a special case of Deployable Output, being the maximum Potential Deployable Output, with no constraints on transmission, pumping, treatment, intake or outlet capacities.

Outage – a temporary loss of Deployable Output due to planned or unplanned events. Planned events are those such as maintenance of sourceworks; unplanned events are exclusively pollution, turbidity, nitrate, algae, power failure and system failure.

Water Available for Use – the Deployable Output of a source less deductions made for allowable outage and planning allowances. This will be the yield figure used for detailed resource planning purposes.

Standards of service

6.   Standards of Service should be linked to control rules to be used in the simulation of the system's operation. For example, one control rule would indicate the storage for the time of year when hosepipe bans should be introduced by the water company. Others could define introductions of bans on non-essential use or rota cuts.

7.   During the simulation, supply is cut back when storage crosses the control rule when drawdown is taking place and supply is increased when the control level is crossed on recovery of storage.

---

1   Deployable Output should **not** be constrained by the cost of operating the system.

8.   The standards of service appropriate to the simulation are the frequencies with which restrictions are required. If the frequencies of restrictions are high then the Deployable Output is increased and vice-versa.

Restrictions in supply

9.   Theit will be necessary to quantify the cut-backs in supply when supply restrictions are imposed in the simulation. The actual supply restrictions imposed and the amount of cut-backs are likely to vary between companies and regions of the country. Typical ranges for the following restrictions, where appropriate, will need to be specified based on historic experience or detailed assumptions:

- voluntary restrictions;
- hosepipe bans;
- non-essential use;
- rota cuts/standpipes (although these are clearly not acceptable to the majority of consumers).

Control rules

10.   Control rules for some systems can be complex and it is not appropriate to specify how they should be calculated. In some cases a trial and error approach may be necessary.

Emergency storage

11.   'Emergency Storage' is a reserve storage aimed at accommodating the **operational** uncertainty regarding the duration of a particular drought and should be allowed for in calculating surface water yields. In practice an operator cannot run the risk that a drought will be no more severe than has been experienced in the

historical or extended historical record. Emergency Storage is calculated as the volume of water required to meet a specified demand for a certain number of days.

123.   The number of days to use is a function of what other emergency back-up is available to the supply system and on analysis of dates associated with the historic end of droughts. The assumption is subjective. A typical value of Emergency Storage might be 30 days of supply but could be more or less depending on reservoir characteristics.

Environmental impact

13.   The impact of a system's operation on the environment is a key factor in calculating the Deployable Output. A number of factors would need to be taken into account in deriving the frequency at which environmental impact might be acceptable. In broad terms, the more severe the drought then the greater the impact which the Environment Agency would be prepared to accept that the aquatic environment should undergo.

Auditability

14.   The impact of a system's operation on the environment is a key factor in calculating the Deployable Output. Normally, the yield of the system will be calculated within the existing licence conditions, but exceptions may be possible by prior arrangement with the Environment Agency, in consultation with other parties where necessary.

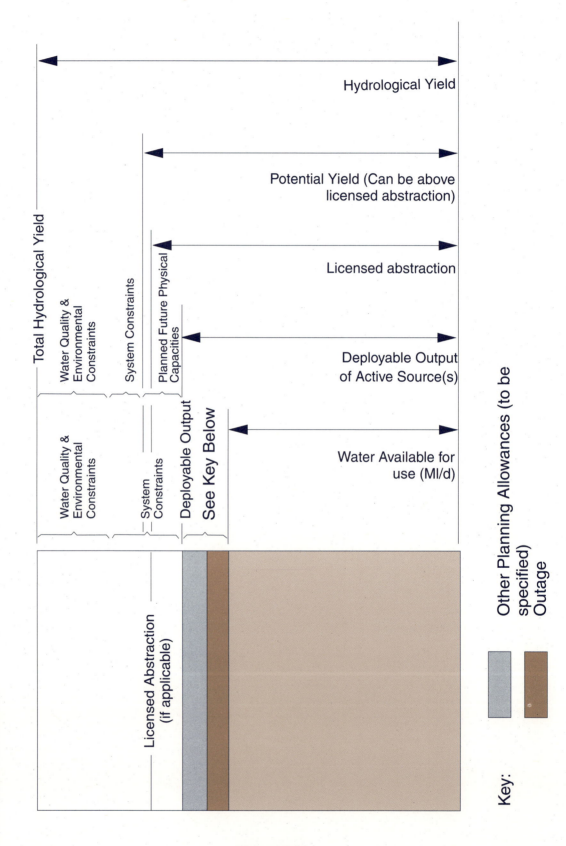

Figure 1. Terms used in the definitions of the output of an active source or group of active sources

STANDARDS OF BEST PRACTICE FOR DEMAND ANALYSIS AND FORECASTING

Introduction

1.   The purpose of this annex, contributed by the Environment Agency, is to outline a series of approaches to public water supply demand forecasting which can generally be regarded as representing standards of best practice given current knowledge and technology. The current 'state of the art' is broadly represented by the output of a recent joint water industry project on demand forecasting methodologies and the following sections summarise the salient aspects of this research. This annex is therefore not intended to present a detailed treatment of demand forecasting best practice and should be read in conjunction with the full report (UKWIR/NRA, 1995) on which it is based. **The approach set out in this annex is open to further consultation and development with the water industry and independent expert organisations, particularly in the light of the material presented in the main report.** Comments should be sent by **6 December 1996** to: The Director of Water Management, The Environment Agency, Rio House, Waterside Drive, Aztec West, Almondsbury, Bristol, BS12 4UD.

Methodology

2.   In October 1995, UK Water Industry Research (UKWIR) and the National Rivers Authority published the results of a joint project commissioned to specify a general framework for the production of public water supply demand forecasts (UKWIR/NRA, 1995). The twelve-month study produced the following main outputs:

◆   an agreed definition of the components of demand for forecasting purposes;

◆   a range of 'acceptable' methodologies for estimating or forecasting each component of demand;

◆   implied 'best practice' techniques for estimating or forecasting each component of demand; and

◆   a standardspreadsheet model for compiling and analysing demand forecasts based on best practice.

General forecasting principles

3.   In addition to the outputs listed above the study was also successful in achieving broad industry agreement to a range of overarching principles which should be considered for all forecasting initiatives. These are outlined in the sections which follow.

Type of analysis

4.   All forecasting should be carried out on the basis of individual components of demand rather than simple 'straight line' estimates of total demand. The level of detail of components should be appropriate for the purpose of the forecast but it should normally be at least sufficient to distinguish each component from Distribution Input down to the level of Consumption and Underground Supply Pipe Losses (see Figure 1). If required, components of raw water can also be determined so that forecasts of Distribution Input can be translated into forecasts of abstraction.

5.   Demand forecasting initiatives should be concentrated on accurate determination of the largest components of demand, those subject to the greatest uncertainty and those that are likely to grow significantly in the future.

6.   Forecasts should be prepared to cover a range of scenarios in which the effects of factors such as prolonged hot summers, different growth rate assumptions, demand management measures and population changes are modelled. This should also include justified assumptions about climate change.

Demand conditions

7.   Forecast scenarios should start from a base year which is not distorted by abnormal conditions either in weather or supply operations. To achieve this may require the use of a normalised base year water balance which has been produced to represent the demand in an "average" year. Any normalisation procedure should follow the recommendations in the UKWIR/NRA methodology and in so doing will be auditable.

8.   The central or best estimate demand forecast scenario should be prepared under the assumption of 'average' weather conditions, with weather-related demand under such conditions implicit in the forecast. In part, the problem of weather-related fluctuations is overcome by the use of peak demand assessments as a basis for many operational and capital plan decisions. Defined peak demands should be assessed in relation to each forecast scenario produced. Peak factors should, where possible, be specific to each major component of demand.

Annex F

Contributed by the Environment Agency

Demand definitions

9.   The standard breakdown of demand for forecasting purposes is given in Figure 1 and should be adhered to within the constraints of available data.

10.   In addition to the definitions in Figure 1, the combination of Underground Supply Pipe Losses and Distribution Losses is termed **Total Leakage**. The combination of Underground Supply Pipe Losses, Distribution Losses and Total Plumbing Losses is termed **Total Treated Water Losses**.

Auditability

11.   A key feature of the UKWIR/Environment Agency Demand Forecasting Methodology is the requirement to demonstrate openly the assumptions and specific techniques applied in producing a forecast. The spreadsheet accompanying the methodology has the facility to produce outputs which would allow external verification of the techniques, assumptions and data sources used. Using this facility any forecast produced can be duplicated, and therefore checked, by a third party. The methodology was designed to be both transparent and auditable and this principle should be extended to its use.

Other considerations

12.   The importance of accurate start year water balance estimates cannot be overstated. It is important that the overall water balance in the base year should be reconciled with leakage estimated from night flow measurement. The suggested water balance reconciliation methodology (Maximum Likelihood Estimation – MLE) should be used to achieve auditable resolution of any water balance closure errors[1]. However, adjustment of measured Distribution Input through the use of MLE should be avoided if possible. Closure errors of greater than 5% of Measured Distribution Input should be investigated thoroughly with a view to improving the water balance reconciliation in future years.

13.   It is important to ensure the consistency of demand forecasts at a number of levels, for example between zone level and company wide forecasts; between occupancy rates and per capita consumption for different customer groups and for customers as a whole. The methodology offers clear guidance on achieving this consistency.

14.   A current demand forecast should be reviewed and, if necessary, revised annually. As part of the review process, forecasts should be monitored both in overall terms, and on the basis of individual components of demand.

Approaches to forecasting

15.   The UKWIR/Environment Agency demand forecasting study presented recommendations on the range of approaches or techniques which could be applied to the assessment of each component of demand or forecast parameter. The relative precision and reliability of each approach was indicated and the following tables summarise the available data sources or methods. Those which were determined to be of highest precision and reliability and which, by definition, could be considered to represent best practice when producing forecasts for planning purposes are shown highlighted. Those methods marked with an asterisk are NOT recommended for any forecasting purposes.

Customer Information

Initial Population Estimates

Source	Relative Precision	Reliability Band
Local Councils	Medium/High	A
Census Agency	Medium/High	A
OPCS	Medium	A

Initial Property Estimates

Source	Relative Precision	Reliability Band
Billing Records	High	A

---

1   There is often a disparity between the distribution input as given by a treatment works meter, and that given by building up distribution input from individual components of demand. This is due to uncertainties in unmeasured demand and leakage; the latter can be underestimated at the expense of the former.

Forecast of Future Population

Source	Relative Precision	Reliability Band
Combination of sources below	High	A
Local Councils	High/Medium	B
OPCS	Medium	B
Census Agency	Medium	B

Forecast of Future Properties

Source	Relative Precision	Reliability Band
Combination of sources below	High	A
DoE Household projections	Medium	B
Local Councils	Medium	B

Major Components of Initial Water Balance

Unmeasured Household Consumption

Method	Relative Precision	Reliability Band
Company Specific Consumption Monitor	Medium/High	A
Other Company Consumption Monitor	Medium	B
Micro-component analysis	Medium/Low	C
Continuous District Metered Area monitoring	Medium/Low	C
Same as measured households	Low	D
Residual in water balance*	Low	D

Unmeasured Non-Household Consumption

Method	Relative Precision	Reliability Band
Micro Component Analysis	Medium	A
Matching to measured customers	Medium/Low	B
Industry Average	Low	D
Residual in water balance*	Low	D

Distribution Losses and supply pipe leakage[2]

Method	Relative Precision	Reliability Band
Combination	High	A
Widespread Nightflow Tests	Medium/High	A
Continuous District Metered Area Monitoring	Medium/High	A
National Leakage Initiative Models	Medium	B
Residual in water balance	Low	C

Major Components of Demand Forecasts

Unmeasured Household Consumption

Method	Relative Precision	Reliability Band
Micro Component Analysis	High	A
Constant growth rate	Medium	B

---

2   Estimates of distribution losses and supply pipe leakage in future years should be consistent with company leakage targets.

Annex F

Contributed by the Environment Agency

Measured Household Consumption

Source	Relative Precision	Reliability Band
Micro Component Analysis	High	A
Constant % of unmeasured	Medium/Low	C
Constant growth rate	Medium/Low	C
Same growth as unmeasured	Medium/Low	C

Measured Non-Household Consumption

Source	Relative Precision	Reliability Band
Economic Forecast	Medium/High	A
Constant growth rate	Medium/Low	B
Consultation with Large Users	Medium	Will improve accuracy of other methods

Reference

UKWIR/NRA, 1995. UKWIR/NRA *Demand Forecasting Methodology Main Report*. September 1995

Figure 1. Demand Forecasting Components.

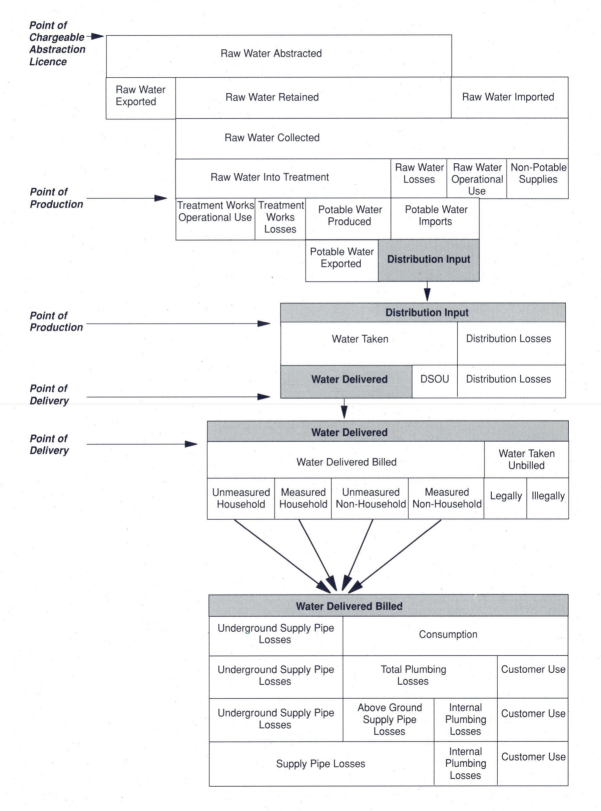

Annex G
Contributed by Ofwat

PROMOTING THE EFFICIENT USE OF WATER BY CUSTOMERS

Introduction

1.   Contributed by the Office of Water Services (Ofwat), this annex discusses some questions that should be asked of companies' policies and practices in promoting the efficient use of water by customers. **The views expressed are those of Ofwat and are open to further consultation and development, particularly in the light of the material presented in the main report.** Comments should be sent by **17 January 1997** to: The Assistant Director (Costs and Performance), The Office of Water Services, Centre City Tower, 7 Hill Street, Birmingham, B5 4UA.

Enhancing incentives: *does the company have the right sort of incentives in place?*

2.   The most effective incentive for the elimination of waste by customers is for them to pay by reference to the volume used. This not only reduces bills in the short term, but also gives the water company guidance for future investment in water resource availability based on customers' willingness to pay. Leading edge companies will have considered the value to their planning of customers voluntarily opting for meters and will have incentives in place to encourage their installation. Companies with current or foreseeable water resource constraints or temporary restrictions will be actively promoting their schemes, including offering free options, but also taking into account customers' views on other issues such as siting and deferred payment terms.

3.   Leading edge companies will be implementing compulsory metering programmes for customers who make high or adverse seasonal demands on the distribution system.

4.   Leading edge companies will be considering how to replicate the individual choices exercised by metered customers for the substantial majority of domestic customers who pay without reference to volume. Companies will be assessing, in the light of the particular circumstances, whether direct action to alter appliance/equipment utilisation of water is warranted. Successful examples can be drawn from other countries, where direct incentives to replace appliances (such as high volume water closets), equipment or to modify gardening habits have reduced water consumption. As well as deferring investment there are water treatment savings for companies.

Better information: *does the company explain what the problem is and the choices available to customers?*

5.   Leading edge companies will explain to their customers, potential customers and those who act on behalf of customers what the options for meeting demand in the future are, and what rôle restrictions may have to play if nothing changes on the demand side. Customers will need to be convinced, and kept up to date by a planned medium term communications strategy. Information will be regularly reviewed and will contain signposted action to enable customers to follow up advice. However, customers will not be convinced they have a rôle to play if they are not satisfied that the company itself is tackling leakage from its own pipes.

6.   Leading edge companies will also be concerned about the purpose to which water for non-domestic use (including business use) is put. This will include information about water efficiency and where water audits can be obtained.

Action: *does the company have skills which can be used cost effectively to reduce waste?*

7.   Leading edge companies will use their skills to help their customers detect and repair leaking pipework. The service will be linked with clear advice for customers about how to test for the possibility of a leak, or with its own billing records to identify relatively high consumptions. Water company action should reflect the need to repair the burst, and an option to spread the cost will already be in place. For companies imposing restrictions on use, serious consideration will have been given to operating a free leak detection and repair service.

The market for water conservation ideas: *are water companies benefitting from the contribution of others?*

8.   There is a sizeable commercial interest in water conservation techniques and products which requires a better focus. Leading edge companies will want to ensure that innovations are translated into action which improves the efficiency of water use and reduces waste. Parallels have been drawn with work of the Energy Savings Trust and the network of local energy advice centres. Leading edge companies will consider how sharing ideas and funding independent advice to the public about water efficiency will improve the effectiveness of their strategies.

METERING AND TARIFFS

Introduction

1.   Contributed by the Office of Water Services (Ofwat), this annex discusses some questions that should be asked of companies' policies and practices in respect of metering and setting tariff structures. Annex C is also relevant to this discussion. **The views expressed in this annex are those of Ofwat and are open to further consultation and development, particularly in the light of the material presented in the main report.** Comments should be sent by **17 January 1997** to: The Assistant Director (Costs and Performance), The Office of Water Services, Centre City Tower, 7 Hill Street, Birmingham, B5 4UA.

Meter option scheme: *does the company have a satisfactory scheme?*

2.   All companies have a meter option scheme and customers with unmeasured supplies can opt for a meter at any time. The cost of fitting a meter and any other conditions must be reasonable, so there should be no disincentive which would deter customers from switching to metering. Where the supply demand balance is tight, leading companies offer very low cost or free meter option schemes. Leading companies are effective in the publication and promotion of their meter option schemes.

Metering new properties: *does the company meter all new connections?*

3.   Leading companies meter all new properties as a matter of course and charge on the basis of metered consumption. Boundary boxes capable of taking meters will be installed when service pipes or stop taps are replaced and the customers involved will be offered the meter option scheme or a free meter.

Metering non-households: *does the company have a fully metered non-household customer base?*

4.   Leading companies will be metering all their non-household properties where it is practical to do so and charging on the basis of metered consumption. In the very few situations where metering is not feasible, leading companies will have developed alternative means of charging, probably based on assessed consumption levels. In these instances leading companies will monitor consumption in the local supply zone to maintain a check that the assessed consumption levels are realistic.

High volume users: *does the company meter them?*

5.   Leading companies will have programmes in place to meter all high volume users – for example those who use garden sprinklers or make other high non-domestic use of water, with a focus on those in supply zones where the supply demand balance is tightest.

Focused compulsory metering programmes: *in areas where the balance between supply and demand is tight, does the company have a focused compulsory metering programme?*

6.   Leading companies will have compulsory metering programmes in place in those supply zones where there would otherwise be or are likely to be insufficient supplies to cater for unmeasured demands without recourse to formal restrictions on water use.

Tariff structures: *does the company have tariffs that reflect costs and help customers?*

7.   Tariff structures should provide:
- **fairness and equity**, to ensure that customers in similar circumstances pay similar charges and that, where they face different bills, the differences in charges properly reflect relevant differences in circumstances;
- **sensible incentives** to customers and to companies, to help ensure that the right level of service is provided at the right price; and
- **simplicity and comprehensibility**, so that customers are clear about how their overall bill is made up and what they can do to influence it.

8.   Leading company charging policies will have a soundly-based balance between tariffs which are simple and cheap to operate and those which are more complex but more closely tailored to the circumstances of individual customers.

Standing charges and volume-related rate: *do the company's charging policies achieve the right balance between standing charges and volume-related charges?*

9.   Leading companies will have tariffs structured so that changes in consumption which result in changes in costs incurred by the company are reflected in customers' bills. These provide customers with the right incentives for economic behaviour. In normal circumstances tariffs would neither encourage excessive use of water nor dictate too little use of water. These companies will have set standing charges to recover only

Annex H

Contributed by Ofwat

those costs relating to the number of customers (currently a maximum of £22 for metered household customers) and for the volume-related rate to reflect the additional costs which companies will incur over the longer term in meeting demand from measured customers. Leading companies will have examined whether their volumetric charges are at the appropriate level, depending on local circumstances. Leading companies will have taken account of environmental costs when calculating charges.

Volume-related tariffs: *has the company considered adopting more sophisticated volume-related tariffs to manage its balance between supply and demand more effectively?*

10. Leading companies with difficulties in maintaining continuity of supplies in either the short or longer term will be considering with all their customers (industrial, commercial and household) more sophisticated volume-related tariffs. Even with simple volume-related tariffs, the reductions in demand and improvements in system efficiency have been very significant. More sophisticated tariffs would achieve better demand management and/or the greater revenues necessary to expand the productive capacity of the infrastructure. Rising block and seasonal volume-related tariffs are said to have had a dramatic effect on water consumption in other countries [as discussed in Annex C]. Significant developments in more sophisticated volume-related tariffs will require reliable data loggers or remotely-readable meters. The potential fluctuations in revenue between dry and wet summers and the increased potential for billing disputes will require careful consideration before peakload pricing can be regarded as practical.

LEAKAGE ASSESSMENT AND REDUCTION

Introduction

1. Contributed by the Office of Water Services (Ofwat), this annex discusses some questions that should be asked of companies' policies and practices in respect of the assessment of leakage from water systems and its reduction to economic levels. **The views expressed in this annex are those of Ofwat and are open to further consultation and development, particularly in the light of the material presented in the main report.** Comments should be sent by **17 January 1997** to: The Assistant Director (Costs and Performance), The Office of Water Services, Centre City Tower, 7 Hill Street, Birmingham, B5 4UA.

2. Assessing the level of leakage from a water system is an inherently difficult process. Since most households are not metered, companies cannot simply measure what goes into their systems against what is delivered to consumers. For the foreseeable future, leakage will have to be estimated by accounting for the water balance and by reconciling the results with data from measuring night flows in supply zones. Even if all companies were at the economic level of leakage, there would be significant differences in the absolute levels due to the different characteristics of company supply areas and the costs of alternative water supplies to their locality.

The water balance: *does the company have a robust and convincing understanding of its current water balance and constituent elements?*

3. Leading edge companies will have a full understanding of the current and future patterns of demand for water. This will be based on the Water Balance (or Integrated Flow) method which measures and estimates all other components and deduces leakage from the residual. These companies will measure flows through their systems continuously and accurately. They will have the systems necessary to provide robust estimates of components of their water balance which are not directly measured. They will use household consumption monitoring systems to help estimate accurately unmeasured household consumption and how it varies over time. They will make use of the increasing body of information on consumption by metered households. They will use the Night Flow method to test some of their critical assumptions. All such information will be used in an integrated way to give them a full understanding of (i) the critical components of water usage by customers both for domestic and also for non-domestic purposes; and (ii) losses within their networks. The information will also be used to make performance comparisons within companies.

4. Leading companies will also test their assumptions against those of other companies. They will ensure there is a robust and persuasive rationale behind any assumptions that are not consistent with those other companies who exhibit exemplary water balance characteristics.

Operational practices: *does the company manage the day to day operation of its infrastructure in an efficient and economic way, particularly with respect to leakage control?*

5. The operational practices in leading companies will encompass all of the following:

♦ **continuous monitoring** of water in their systems from sources right through to the distribution systems and down to relatively small and discrete district meter zones;

♦ **static 'drop tests'** carried out regularly on all service reservoirs and gravity aqueducts;

♦ **effective display** of this data into real time operational information accessible to those staff responsible for the interface with customers as well as to executive management thus enabling prompt and timely action by all responsible parties;

♦ **routine Night Line flow measurement** in the majority of supply zones to enable identification of changes in either consumption by customers or previously undetected leakage;

♦ focused use of pressure control to reduce high pressure (and hence high leakage) both permanently and at different times of the day without causing concern to their customers, particularly those who have installed direct water heating systems (the exemplary company will have identified these customers within their systems);

♦ **sufficient leakage control teams** to ensure full coverage of their supply areas on a regular cycle;

♦ **accurate cost allocation** to ensure that the full costs of their day to day activities are recorded, accessible to facilitate comparisons between districts, teams *etc.* and to provide a basis for the regular review of the economic level of leakage control; and

♦ **quick response burst repair teams** to ensure prompt attention to major bursts and those impacting on thecontinuity of supplies to any customer(s), with resources sufficient to attend to smaller bursts within a reasonable period particularly those reported by customers.

Annex I

Contributed by Ofwat

6.   In time of water shortage leading companies will increase their activities in the above areas to ensure that all that can be done to safeguard supplies is done and that customers can see the efforts being made. During water shortages, customer confidence in the efficiency and effectiveness of their water company is imperative.

Economic levels of leakage: *is the company operating, or taking adequate steps to operate, at the economic levels of leakage?*

7.   In a leading company, expenditure on leakage control would be increased to the point where the incremental costs involved in maintaining the current level of leakage in each discrete supply area are in balance with the long run incremental costs of the cheapest alternative for balancing supply and demand (metering, more sophisticated volume-related tariffs, resource development *etc*.). The long run costs would include environmental costs and/or benefits even if these are not borne directly by the company.

8.   Methods have been developed over a number of years to assist companies in both assessing their economic level of leakage and guide implementation of effective leakage control to achieve and maintain such a state (UK Water Industry, 1994). Leading companies will take such methods and apply them in a robust and proper way that stands independent scrutiny.

9.   Leading companies will be able to convince their customers, regulators and politicians that they are operating and maintaining the economic levels of leakage control. Until such time all companies will be required to report regularly on their performance, especially those that need to demonstrate they are operating their systems at economic levels of leakage. The regulator will scrutinise and publish his assessment of each individual company's performance, seeking rapid corrective action where this is appropriate. Poorly performing companies will have leakage targets imposed upon them by the regulator if this is considered necessary.

Reference

UK Water Industry, 1994. *Managing Leakage*. WRc plc/Water Services Association/Water Companies Association, 1994.

CONTINUITY AND SECURITY OF SUPPLY ISSUES

Introduction

1.   Contributed by the Office of Water Services, this annex identifies the general questions that should be asked of companies' policies and practices in respect of the identification of costs and benefits of different levels of security of supply and in establishing customers views on the balance to be struck on these. **The views expressed in this annex are those of Ofwat and are open to further consultation and development, particularly in the light of the material presented in the main report.** Comments should be sent by **17 January 1997** to: The Assistant Director (Costs and Performance), The Office of Water Services, Centre City Tower, 7 Hill Street, Birmingham, B5 4UA.

The water balance: *does the company have a robust and convincing understanding of its current water balance and constituent elements?*

2.   Leading edge companies will have a full understanding of the current patterns of demand for water. These companies will measure flows through their systems continuously and accurately. They will have robust systems to provide good estimates of each component of their water balance. They will use household consumption monitoring systems to help estimate accurately unmeasured domestic consumption and how it varies over time. They will make use of the increasing body of information on consumption by metered households. Such information will be used in an integrated way, to give them a full understanding of the critical components of water usage by customers and losses within networks.

The water infrastructure and tariffs: *does the company manage its water infrastructure and charging schemes in an efficient and effective way that both optimises delivery of water services and provide incentives for efficient behaviour by customers?*

3.   Leading edge companies will be able to demonstrate prudent and efficient management of the water infrastructure for both today's and tomorrow's customers. These companies will manage their systems to contain leakage at economic levels. Their performance will be evident from their own visible activities and by comparison with other companies in the regular reporting and publication of statistics by the respective regulators.

4.   These companies will have a fair charging scheme for their customers. Every opportunity will be taken to increase the measured customer base through opportunistic, targeted and low cost optional metering schemes and selective metering. Tariffs will reflect costs of supply in both normal and abnormal supply conditions. There will be no significant discrimination between different classes of customers in terms of charging or domestic service provision. Exemplar companies will provide prompt and appropriate compensation to customers who do not receive the full normal service due to extreme circumstances.

5.   Leading edge companies will understand fully the current productive capacity of existing water resources and how this may change over time. They will have considered and made contingency plans for drought periods and for the implications of climatic change on their productive capacity.

The costs of delivery: *does the company have a proper allocation and understanding of both the short- and long-run costs of delivery of water services?*

6.   A leading edge company will have robust systems for understanding and reporting its total and unit costs of supply in each distinct system and over time. The costs will be monitored regularly to ensure the efficient operation of its systems in both the short and long term. These companies will understand the total and unit cost implications of each possible shift in their internal policy or practice.

The forecasting of trends and influences: *does the company have a sound information base for forecasting trends in the water balance components based on a full understanding of the patterns of demand, patterns of supply, and consumer attitudes?*

7.   Leading edge companies will have a robust basis for assessing the balance between supply and demand over the longer term. They will have done work on the likely patterns of demand and what their customers will want to use water for in the future. They will have taken due note of exogenous social and economic factors. For example, they will have identified and quantified the changes taking place in the relevant patterns of behaviour, like showering and gardening.

8.   These companies will be investigating the price customers are willing to pay for different uses at different times. These investigations will be structured in-

volving best practices for such market research. From such work exemplar companies will understand what level of service their customers want and what value they place on different levels of service.

9.   These companies will have identified certain groups of customers who are prepared to pay a higher price in exchange for a higher level or quantity of service, and then provided this choice for them through appropriate tariffs and measuring systems. If increases in overall volumes of water delivered are sought by customers then the additional monies from the extra sales will provide for any necessary expansion of the system without recourse to increases in general price levels.

10.   Leading edge companies would have used all these tools to ensure their operations, charging policies and procurement of new assets are optimised to ensure continuity of supplies to their customers both now and in the future. In so doing such a company will have earned the confidence and co-operation of its customers and the public through a record of high service performance at a fair price.

Learning Resources
Centre

Printed in the United Kingdom for The Stationery Office
Dd 302688   C15   10/96   362176   40/36479